Treating Traumatic Stress in Adults

Treating Traumatic Stress in Adults is a resource for therapists of all disciplines for use in the treatment of adults suffering from post-traumatic stress. By reading this unique synthesis of information on the most current trauma treatments and expressive writing exercises, practitioners will gain an integrative and practical set of tools for treating post-traumatic stress. Also included are numerous diverse case vignettes, exercises for building trust in the patient/client relationship, and sections dedicated to exploring the client's thought patterns and emotions to provide an opportunity for exposure, healing, and restructuring maladaptive beliefs.

Stephanie Field, PsyD, is a licensed clinical psychologist at the Counseling and Psychological Services department at the University of Hartford and sits on the Board of Directors for the Connecticut Psychological Association. She has worked primarily with adults and young adults, specializing in substance use disorders, traumatic stress, and expressive writing therapy.

Kathy McCloskey, PhD, PsyD, ABPP-CL, is a research psychologist, a licensed clinical psychologist, a Diplomate of the American Board of Professional Psychology, and a professor at the University of Hartford Graduate Institute of Professional Psychology in Hartford, CT. She is the co-author of two books (*Backs Against the Wall: Battered Women's Resistance Strategies* and *A Sexuality and Gender Diversity Training Program*), and has published over 70 peer-reviewed scholarly papers over her 30-plus year professional career. Her specialties include feminist psychology, multicultural and diversity issues, intimate partner violence, trauma, forensic populations, and the training of doctoral-level clinical psychologists.

Treating Traumatic Stress in Adults
The Practitioner's Expressive Writing Workbook

Stephanie Field and Kathy McCloskey

NEW YORK AND LONDON

First published 2016
by Routledge
711 Third Avenue, New York, NY 10017

and by Routledge
2 Park Square, Milton Park, Abingdon, Oxon, OX14 4RN

Routledge is an imprint of the Taylor & Francis Group, an informa business

© 2016 Taylor & Francis

The right of Stephanie Field and Kathy McCloskey to be identified as authors of this work has been asserted by them in accordance with sections 77 and 78 of the Copyright, Designs and Patents Act 1988.

All rights reserved. No part of this book may be reprinted or reproduced or utilised in any form or by any electronic, mechanical, or other means, now known or hereafter invented, including photocopying and recording, or in any information storage or retrieval system, without permission in writing from the publishers.

Trademark notice: Product or corporate names may be trademarks or registered trademarks, and are used only for identification and explanation without intent to infringe.

Library of Congress Cataloging-in-Publication Data

Field, Stephanie Leigh.
Treating traumatic stress in adults: the practitioner's expressive writing workbook / Stephanie Field and Kathy McCloskey.
  pages cm
Includes bibliographical references and index.
  1. Post-traumatic stress disorder—Treatment. 2. Psychic trauma—Treatment.
  I. McCloskey, Kathy A. II. Title.
RC552.P67F53 2015
616.85'21—dc23

2015018305

ISBN: 978-1-138-89075-6 (hbk)
ISBN: 978-1-138-89076-3 (pbk)
ISBN: 978-1-315-71007-5 (ebk)

Typeset in Sabon
by codeMantra

*On that glad night
in secret, for no one saw me,
nor did I look at anything
with no other light or guide
than the one that burned in my heart.*
—St. John of the Cross, *"The Dark Night"*

To the patient souls whose secrets are unwritten and unspoken. It is for those looking for their light at the edge of darkness to illuminate that which is hidden from others and most importantly from themselves.

Contents

PART I
Introduction: Integrating Expressive Writing Into
Trauma-Related Treatment Approaches 1

Trauma and Its Effects 3

Implications for Treatment 10

PART II
Current Treatments for Trauma 13

Discussion of a Multidimensional Model 23

Future Treatment: The Case for Including Expressive Writing . . . 25

Expressive Writing as a Therapy Technique 31

Conclusion 39

PART III
Expressive Writing Workbook 43

General Writing Guidelines 43

Structuring Client Writing Activities during Session 44

PART III-I
Beginning Exercises 47

Section 1: Lists and Clusters 47

Section 2: Sentence Stems 56

Section 3: Acrostics and Poems ... 66

Section 4: Five-Minute "Sprints" ... 73

PART III-II
Intermediate Exercises ... 78

Section 1: Letters ... 78

Section 2: Obituaries and Eulogies ... 81

Section 3: Character Sketches ... 85

Section 4: Dialogues ... 88

PART III-III
Advanced Exercises ... 91

Section 1: Narratives ... 91

Section 2: Essays and Compositions ... 96

PART III-IV
Free-Writing Exercises ... 106

Exercise 1: Semiautomatic Writing ... 106

Exercise 2: Into the Stream ... 107

PART III-V
Activity-Based Exercises ... 108

Section 1: Relaxation Exercises ... 108

Section 2: Guided Imagery ... 110

Section 3: Multimedia Activities ... 116

PART III-VI
Outcome Measures ... 121

Rationale ... 121

Screen for Post-traumatic Stress Symptoms ... 121

The Revised Helping Alliance Questionnaire (HAq-II) 121

Alternate Measures for the Assessment of Trauma Symptoms 122

Process 126

Appendix A: SPTSS 127
Appendix B: The Revised Helping Alliance Questionnaire (HAq-II) 129
References 133
Index 143

Part I

Introduction
Integrating Expressive Writing Into Trauma-Related Treatment Approaches

Given the prevalence of violence and trauma within the U.S., psychologists have become increasingly involved with treating individuals who are suffering from traumatic stress. The effects of trauma pose a problem of great magnitude due to their far-reaching impact on society. Suggesting that trauma has costly intergenerational effects, Widom and Maxfield (1996) found that half of those arrested for criminal offenses by the age of 32 had been the victims of abuse and neglect (as cited in Streeck-Fischer & van der Kolk, 2000). In support of the link between trauma history and substance abuse, Ford and Smith (2008) found that 91% of 231 men and women in outpatient substance abuse disorder treatment met criteria for Post-traumatic stress disorder (PTSD). This suggests that trauma has profound and costly consequences for society.

Current treatments for trauma (e.g., cognitive-behavioral, body work, psychodynamic, narrative therapy) share various elements. Schottenbauer, Arnkoff, Glass, and Gray (2006) found a great deal of commonality in trauma treatment approaches used by therapists from divergent self-identified orientations (i.e., cognitive-behavioral or psychodynamic). This commonality may be partially due to the finding that there was a great deal of heterogeneity in how treatment was conducted among therapists from a particular orientation. Therapists who identified as coming from solely a cognitive-behavioral or psychodynamic background reported using more integrative therapy with clients suffering from PTSD. Commonality in treatment approach was not only found among therapists of different theoretical orientations, but also within treatment for clients reporting different trauma histories. Schottenbauer et al. found that treatment did not differ due to the type of trauma reported (e.g., single vs. complex). It seems that therapists tend to practice in certain ways regardless of theoretical orientation or types of trauma history.

What does this suggest about the future of psychotherapy for trauma? Because therapists have an overall propensity to blend techniques (including when treating trauma patients), it seems that deliberately integrated treatment may be an attractive and optimal approach. Schottenbauer et al. (2006) argue that treatment may need to be more broadly focused than the previously developed manualized therapies in order to optimize patient care. Therefore, there seems to be a need for integrative treatment that allows therapists to deliver more comprehensive services.

The present effort brings to bear the world of artistic expression to current treatments for traumatic stress so as to create an integrative, unified approach. Artistic expression in the form of expressive writing is a multifaceted tool in the treatment of traumatic stress. Expressive writing provides information on client thoughts and emotions (Chavis, 2011), allowing the reassessment of maladaptive beliefs (Hynes & Hynes-Berry, 2011). Writing is not only an avenue for emotional catharsis and healing post-trauma; it can serve as an excellent vehicle with which to deliver exposure to past traumatic stimuli, as well as the associated cognitions and emotions with which many clients deal.

An integrative therapy workbook is presented for therapists to use in the treatment of individuals suffering from post-traumatic stress. The workbook synthesizes knowledge about current treatment for trauma, and creative exercises used in poetry therapy, producing an integrative collection of writing exercises that treat a variety of aspects of post-traumatic stress reactions. Beginning sections include exercises that create a sense of safety and build therapeutic rapport. For example, these exercises teach clients self-regulation skills, guiding them to reflect on their own physical and affective experiences. Later writing exercises explore and reveal clients' thought patterns and emotions, and provide an opportunity for exposure, healing, and restructuring their maladaptive beliefs. For example, to better foster more adaptive thinking patterns, a client may create a poem using his or her "rational" voice. Exercises of this nature are expected to complement extant methods in the treatment of trauma and to add a creative, holistic, depth-oriented dimension to empirically supported treatments. Writing exercises will provide an opportunity for *imaginal exposure* where clients confront traumatic stimuli (e.g., images and thoughts) mentally with the goal of a decrease in post-traumatic stress symptoms (e.g., hyper-arousal, avoidance).

However, it should be noted that indiscriminate use of exposure may have unintended consequences for trauma survivors (Pitman, Altman, Greenwald, & Longpre, 1991; van der Kolk, McFarlane, & van der Hart, 1996). Re-traumatization and worsening of symptoms can occur when certain conditions for such treatment are not met or if the client is not assessed properly. Later sections will discuss the need for clinicians to develop techniques based on careful assessment of the client's tolerance for exposure to traumatic stimuli.

We believe expressive writing can be the central therapy or major adjunct to therapy in the treatment of traumatic stress. To this end, the first section of this effort will describe/summarize research about how trauma affects the brain as well as emotions, cognitions, and behavior. An understanding of the effects of trauma will illuminate how expressive writing can be of use with trauma survivors. The second section will summarize major current treatments for trauma and discuss strengths and weaknesses of these treatments. The case will be made for expressive writing as useful in amplifying the strengths of these treatments and buttressing areas of weakness. Current literature will be reviewed on the usefulness of expressive reading and writing in therapy, and how writing can be integrated in the treatment of traumatic stress. Lastly, a clinician's workbook provides ideas and examples of ways expressive writing can be incorporated into the treatment of traumatic stress. Invoking the words of Edward Stainbrook in the opening chapter of *Poetry in the Therapeutic Experience* (Lerner, 1994, as cited in Lerner, 1997), it is hoped that the merger between poetry therapy and current trauma therapies may result in "the revitalizing and remoralizing of the self by providing a wholeness of consciousness—an integration of emotion, cognition, and imagery—with which to create and maintain personal meaning" (p. 11).

Trauma and Its Effects

The *Diagnostic and Statistical Manual of Mental Disorders, 5th Edition* (*DSM-V*; American Psychiatric Association, 2013), has listed trauma and stressor-related disorders including: (a) Acute Stress Disorder (ASD) and (b) Post-traumatic stress disorder (PTSD). Both require exposure to a traumatic or stressful event for diagnosis and involve the re-experiencing of those events, hyper-arousal, and avoidance (Foa, Cahill, & Pontoski, 2004; van Emmerik, Kamphuis, & Emmelkamp, 2008). Symptoms also include negative alterations in cognitions and mood and may include dissociative symptoms (American Psychiatric Association, 2013). It should be noted that reactions to trauma are widespread, and not everyone who is exposed to trauma goes on to develop ASD or PTSD (Foa et al., 2004; van Emmerik et al., 2008). Furthermore, people can often experience many of the symptoms characteristic of the two disorders without meeting full criteria for either.

Herman (1992), Terr (1990), and van der Kolk (2002) have proposed a complex adaptation to trauma that is not captured by the DSM diagnostic criteria for PTSD. Terr (1990) distinguished between Type I and Type II traumas. Type I trauma would be the result of one traumatic event, whereas Type II involves prolonged and/or repeated exposure to traumatic events. Terr described a Type II syndrome characterized by numbing, dissociation, and alternating between behavioral extremes. Herman also suggested that chronic traumatic stressors can result in what she terms *complex post-traumatic stress disorder*. She stated that reactions to trauma can best be thought of as a "spectrum of conditions rather than as a single disorder" (p. 119). The spectrum would range from a brief stress reaction to a short-term traumatic stressor to a complex syndrome in response to prolonged trauma. Herman described complex PTSD as resulting from a "history of subjection to totalitarian control over a prolonged period (months to years)" (p. 121). Examples include being prisoners of war, concentration-camp survivors, intimate partner violence, and prolonged sexual abuse. Herman also described how complex PTSD involves alterations in affect regulation, consciousness, self-perception, perception of the perpetrator, interpersonal relations, and systems of meaning-making. This constellation of symptoms occurs mainly after exposure to interpersonal trauma at an early age (van der Kolk & Fisler, 1994). The existence of complex PTSD is believed to be a more severe type of PTSD as supported by research such as that of Ford and Smith (2008). Complex PTSD was found to be associated with the co-occurrence of depressive symptoms and more severe levels of trauma than those with simple PTSD (Ford & Smith, 2008). In addition, complex PTSD was found to be co-morbid with substance abuse disorders—they found that of 231 outpatient clients receiving substance abuse treatment, 50% had simple PTSD, while 41% met criteria for both simple and complex PTSD.

Van der Kolk and Courtois (2005) supported the concept of a complex response that results from chronic and/or developmental trauma and define it under the phrase, *disorders of extreme stress not otherwise specified* (DESNOS). DESNOS is conceptualized as alterations in ability to regulate emotions, consciousness, and memory, problematic relations with the perpetrator and others, negative physical/medical status (somatization), and disturbances in systems of meaning-making. A high incidence of such symptoms has been found in individuals with histories of prolonged interpersonal trauma and especially in those with early onset exposure during childhood (van der Kolk, Roth, Pelcovitz, Sunday, & Spinazzola, 2005). Streeck-Fischer and van der Kolk (2000) posited that disturbances in emotional self-regulation are among the most salient effects of experiencing chronic trauma and lead to problems in other areas such as a lack of self-definition, distrust in others, and difficulties with impulse control.

They suggested that the inability to emotionally self-regulate is linked to a deficit in the ability to describe internal states verbally. According to van der Kolk and Courtois, trauma involves pervasive changes in neurochemistry that have far-reaching consequences for emotional and behavioral regulation. This is thought to be particularly true for those with early exposure to trauma, which can negatively impact patterns of dendritic branching in the brain during development and maturation (Streeck-Fischer & van der Kolk, 2000).

Psychobiology of Trauma

To better understand how treatments are effective, it is important to understand the physiological underpinnings of traumatic stress on the individual. Human behavior and thought are clearly not divorced from the body (Grame, Tortorici, Healey, Dillingham, & Winklebaur, 1999), and more comprehensive and holistic treatment approaches should take this into account. Perry

(1999, as cited in Grame et al., 1999), in describing the response to threat to survival, wrote:

> All areas of the brain and body are recruited and orchestrated for optimal survival tasks during the threat. This total neurobiological participation in the threat response is important in understanding how a traumatic experience can impact and alter functioning in such a pervasive fashion. Cognitive, emotional, social, behavioral, and physiological residue of a trauma may impact an individual for years—even a lifetime. (p. 3)

In their study of 27 women with PTSD, Hopper, Frewen, van der Kolk, and Lanius (2007) found that neural activation in different areas of the brain correlated with script-driven trauma imagery and symptoms of re-experiencing, avoidance, and dissociation (Hopper et al., 2007). Specifically, trauma re-experience severity was associated with greater activity in the right anterior insula, an area linked to the somatic aspects of emotional states such as sympathetic arousal (Craig, 2002, as cited in Hopper et al., 2007). In addition, higher levels of trauma re-experiencing were linked with less brain activity in an area associated with the inhibition of amygdala activity and modulation of conditioned emotional responses. Trauma re-experiencing, as well as severity of avoidance and dissociation, was associated with brain activity reflecting less ability to inhibit emotional experience. These findings support the conceptualization of PTSD as a disorder in emotional regulation and a failure over time to extinguish the fear response that has roots in the differential activation of particular areas of the brain. Hopper and colleagues discussed how individuals with PTSD may display pathological emotional over-engagement reflected by hyper-arousal and re-experiencing symptoms or they may display pathological emotional under-engagement involving dissociative symptoms. Other psychobiological changes have been found to be associated with trauma history. These include alterations in cortisol level (Miller, Chen, & Zhou, 2007; Taylor, Weems, Costa, & Carrion, 2009), facial electromyography, heart rate, skin conductance, and blood pressure (Pole, 2007; Wolfe et al., 2000). In addition, changes in vagal regulation have been noted (Porges, 2004). According to Polyvagal Theory, Porges stated that the vagal circuit involves face to heart neural connections where the neural control of the heart is connected anatomically to the neural control of facial and head muscles. Given this connection, disruption to the vagal circuit, as found in trauma, can have a broad impact on emotional regulation and social relatedness by affecting how facial muscles respond to emotional dysregulation. Dale and colleagues (2009) found that women with abuse histories demonstrated less vagal tone (i.e., respiratory sinus arrhythmia) and an inability to quickly re-engage vagal regulation immediately following mild physical exercise. These findings provide evidence for how trauma can affect a person's physiology on a profound level. It appears that a history of trauma prevents the autonomic nervous system from more easily returning to a baseline state after arousal. This can have long-term health consequences, and is related to the ability to regulate emotions and behaviors, as well as the ability to return to a state of less physiological arousal.

Indeed, Dale et al. (2009) cited that poor vagal regulation may be related to psychological dysfunction including social anxiety (Movius & Allen, 2005, as cited in Dale et al.) and may hinder recovery from depression (Rottenberg, Salomon, Gross, & Gotlib, 2005). Dale and colleagues hypothesized that abuse history alters the vagal feedback loop, and decreases the efficiency of the vagal "brake," which promotes trusting interactions and engagement behaviors. Individuals who have less efficient vagal regulation may experience greater levels of hyper-arousal, and have difficulties in their ability to enter into trusting states and intimate interactions.

Van der Kolk and Fisler (1994) discussed how childhood abuse and neglect can also lead to a diminished ability to self-regulate. Survivors of childhood trauma lose the ability to regulate the intensity of emotions, as well as the ability to control impulses. Streeck-Fischer and van der Kolk (2000) noted that the capacity for representational memory (i.e., internalized representations similar to the idea of 'object permanence') is disrupted by trauma, and that this representational memory is crucial to the development of emotional and behavioral regulation.

Representational memory is a function of a developed frontal cortex; decreased frontal lobe functioning is related to an impaired ability to understand the larger context in which a particular event occurs (Streeck-Fischer & van der Kolk, 2000). Cole and Putnam (1986) posited that the loss of self-regulatory functions in abused children leads to identity disturbance, reflected by: (a) disruption in sense of self, (b) inability to regulate affect and impulses, and (c) insecurity in relationships (as cited in van der Kolk & Fisler, 1994).

As the impact of trauma on the central nervous system is determined by maturational level and severity of abuse, chronic abuse and neglect and trauma at younger ages would seem to have more deleterious effects on the brain than would an isolated traumatic event. The impact of trauma on neurochemistry (specifically the limbic system) can manifest in disruptions of emotional and behavioral regulation, as well as impulse control. Such negative disruptions can result in a host of symptoms, including, for example, an increase in aggressive acts (toward the self and others), eating disorders, and substance abuse (van der Kolk & Fisler, 1994).

Disruptions in Emotion-Identification

As mentioned earlier, abused children often exhibit the inability to identify and express their emotions verbally (Streeck-Fischer & van der Kolk, 2000; van der Kolk & Fisler, 1994). It makes sense that among those with traumatic stress, the associated emotional over-arousal, inability to self-regulate, and lack of internalized representations would be linked to deficits in labeling and expressing emotions. Traumatized individuals may fail to recognize emotional states because of overall greater levels of hyper-arousal that prompt fight-or-flight reactions (Streeck-Fischer & van der Kolk, 2000; van der Kolk & Fisler, 1994). Nemiah (1991) and Putnam (1991) suggest that lack of awareness concerning internal states may also relate to dissociation and serve as a coping mechanism in the face of overwhelming stress (as cited in van der Kolk & Fisler, 1994). The idea that trauma hinders the ability to identify and label affective states is supported by Schneider-Rosen and Cicchetti's (1984) research showing that maltreated toddlers use fewer words to describe internal states compared to their non-traumatized peers.

Interestingly, Amir, Stafford, Freshman, and Foa (1998) found that the degree of transcribed narrative articulation shortly after trauma was related to the future severity of PTSD symptoms: less richness and verbosity within the trauma narrative is associated with greater PTSD symptom severity. In addition, Foa, Molnar, and Cashman (1995) found that narratives of sexual assault victims with PTSD at the end of exposure therapy were longer and had a higher percentage of organized thoughts (as cited in Amir et al., 1998). Furthermore, greater cohesion in the narratives was associated with a reduction in trauma related anxiety (Foa et al., 1995, as cited in Amir et al., 1998). Impulsive actions and impaired impulse control have also been associated with difficulty putting feelings into words (Fish-Murray et al., 1987, as cited in van der Kolk & Fisler, 1994). As van der Kolk & Fisler stated, "… when the mind is able to create symbolic representations of these past experiences, there often seems to be a taming of terror: a desomatization of experience" (p. 154). Words can provide the coping strategy necessary to increase a sense of mastery and control.

These findings suggest that trauma may have a negative impact on the neural processes involved with language, memory, social interactions, and understanding complex social patterns due to sensory-perceptual disturbances (Streeck-Fischer & van der Kolk, 2000). Overall, traumatized individuals need to improve their ability to put feelings into words; they also need to create an internal narrative of traumatic experiences replete with symbolic meaning to fully integrate memories of the trauma and reorganize distorted beliefs resulting from the trauma. In this way, trauma survivors can abandon maladaptive behaviors that may once have been quite adaptive. In addition, Streeck-Fischer and van der Kolk asserted that treatment needs to involve symbolic linguistic expression, allow the traumatized individual to try out different social roles and outcomes, and help individuals explore how others might have dealt with feared emotions and past situations. Furthermore, treatment for traumatic stress would need to provide a sense of emotional and behavioral containment that was previously unavailable and create a way for individuals to regulate themselves within such arenas (Streeck-Fischer & van der Kolk, 2000). It is suggested here that the process of expressive writing can provide just such a treatment option to address emotional and behavioral containment for trauma survivors through its structure, pacing, and assistance in self-regulation.

Interpersonal and Cognitive Effects of Trauma

In addition to neurobiological consequences, trauma can negatively affect the interpersonal functioning of individuals on many different levels (Harris & Valentiner, 2002). Traditional talk therapy as an intimate, interpersonal process brings to the fore interpersonal styles and beliefs that have been profoundly affected by trauma. Given this, trauma treatment should take into account the differences and interpersonal limitations of those who are suffering traumatic stress. Specifically, beliefs about the self and the world are altered as a result of traumatic experiences, which can lead to long-term behavioral problems (Foa, Ehlers, Clark, Tolin, & Orsillo, 1999; Janoff-Bulman, 1989; Janoff-Bulman & Frieze, 1983; McCann & Pearlman, 1990). For instance, problematic thought processes and beliefs can negatively affect how individuals relate to each other in close relationships (Owens & Chard, 2001), such as decreasing the level of intimacy (Fehr, 2004). A decrease in intimacy may have important implications for the overall amount of social support received in close relationships (Sanderson, Rahm, Beigbeder, & Metts, 2005).

A cognitive schema can be defined as a mental framework that confirms a core belief about the self, others, or the world. After a traumatic experience, personal schemas are changed to accommodate the realization that horrific events occur in the world (Cason, Resick, & Weaver, 2002; Foa et al., 1999; Owens & Chard, 2001). Almost two decades ago, Janoff-Bulman (1989) and Janoff-Bulman and Frieze (1983) detailed three specific sets of cognitive schemas that are affected by trauma: (a) perceived benevolence of the world, (b) meaningfulness of life and the world, and (c) worthiness of the self. Similarly, Constructivist Self Development Theory (CSDT) specifies five principal areas of schematic change resulting from abuse as they refer to self and to interpersonal relatedness: (a) safety, (b) trust, (c) control, (d) esteem, and (e) intimacy (McCann & Pearlman, 1990; McCann, Sakheim, & Abrahamson, 1988; Pearlman, 2001; Pearlman & Saakvitne, 1995).

There is some agreement that various types of trauma affect different cognitive schemas. Specifically, some traumas mainly change beliefs about the self, while others change beliefs about the world. Foa, Ehlers, Clark, Tolin, and Orsillo (1999) found three sets of schemas that are affected by trauma: (a) negative cognitions about self (general negative view of self), (b) negative cognitions about the world, and (c) self-blame. Owens and Chard (2001) found that female survivors of childhood sexual abuse had altered beliefs regarding self-blame, whereas rape survivors had altered beliefs regarding both self-blame and beliefs about the world. Furthermore, Foa and colleagues found that accident survivors viewed their world more positively than victims of assault because assault was classified as interpersonal trauma as opposed to an accident. In other words, interpersonal trauma more negatively affects how one perceives the world than accident trauma. In sum, the impact of interpersonal trauma on one's perception of the world may have negative implications for psychological well-being in a different way than the experience of accidents or natural disasters.

Harris and Valentiner (2002) found that disruptions in perceived benevolence of the world, meaningfulness of the world, and worthiness of the self are related to fear of intimacy in relationships and thus play an important role in the interpersonal functioning of individuals. They hypothesized that the belief that the world and other people are unsafe, as well as the belief that the self is unworthy, would lead individuals to avoid intimate relationships (Harris & Valentiner, 2002). Results indicate that the view of one's self and the world, as well as depressive symptoms, did indeed predict fear of intimacy in relationships. Similarly, McEwan, de Man, and Simpson-Housley (2002) found that survivors of rape had greater fear of intimacy than women who had not experienced sexual assault. Davis, Petretic-Jackson, and Ting's (2001) research further indicated that women who had experienced multiple abuse (physical and sexual) during childhood reported greater fear of intimacy than women who had undergone a single type of abuse or no abuse. In addition, women who had reported a single type of abuse did not differ significantly from women who had no abuse history in terms of fear of intimacy, suggesting that the experience of multiple types of abuse is significant in predicting avoidance of intimate relationships (Davis et al., 2001).

Trauma can also disrupt patterns of relating that foster intimacy and relationship satisfaction by altering cognitive schemas and affecting psychological well-being (Harris & Valentiner, 2002). McCann and colleagues (1988) noted a variety of psychological responses as a result of cognitive distortions involving one's self and the world. These included anxiety, social withdrawal, and fear of betrayal, which can greatly hinder social intimacy in the life of the trauma survivor. The World Assumptions Scale (WAS) can assess these changed beliefs by measuring assumptions about the self, others, and the world (Janoff-Bulman, 1989). Subscales on the WAS include: the benevolence of the world (e.g., "The world is a good place"), the benevolence of people (e.g., "People are basically kind and helpful"), justice (e.g., "Misfortune is least likely to strike worthy, decent people"), control (e.g., "Through our actions we can prevent bad things from happening to us"), self-worth (e.g., "I am very satisfied with the kind of person I am"), personal control ("I take the actions necessary to protect myself against misfortune"), and luck ("I am basically a lucky person"). Low agreement with such dimensions on the WAS correlated with depression and fearful attitudes toward relationships, thus pointing toward the role trauma plays in affecting post-traumatic emotions and interpersonal functioning (Janoff-Bulman, 1989; Janoff-Bulman & Frieze, 1983). In Wenninger and Ehlers' (1998) study, highly reinforced patterns of thinking were also related to post-traumatic symptoms in survivors of childhood sexual abuse; for instance, maladaptive beliefs about safety, trust, self-esteem, and intimacy were associated with higher post-traumatic symptom scores (Wenninger & Ehlers, 1998).

It appears that trauma can also change beliefs about the self by engendering feelings of guilt and self-blame. For example, Fehr (2004) found that speaking about personal trauma can create a sense of guilt and discomfort for the survivor, while De Francis (1969) found that more than the actual childhood sexual abuse itself, disclosure of the abuse brought about a sense of guilt for 64% of victims queried. Both authors found that victims felt guilty not only from confessing the childhood sexual victimization, but for having been involved in the occurrence; feelings of guilt on the part of the victim were also accompanied by feelings of anxiety and lowered self-esteem (De Francis, 1969; Fehr, 2004). These outcomes of childhood sexual abuse may have an impact on a victim's capacity to self-disclose and therefore to increase safety or maintain close relationships.

Lower inclinations to self-disclose may affect the development of relationships because self-disclosure is integral to the development of intimacy (Sanderson et al., 2005). Sanderson and colleagues (2005) found that individuals who were willing to engage in personal self-disclosure experienced greater satisfaction in relationships. Furthermore, these individuals maintained relationships that provided greater levels of social support, and they maintained them over longer periods of time (Sanderson et al., 2005).

We can hypothesize that cognitive schemas relating to the self and others interfere with the tendency to self-disclose, thereby decreasing intimacy and satisfaction in trauma survivors. In addition to self-disclosure, trauma may also disrupt general beliefs about relationships and have negative consequences on interpersonal functioning that might promote intimacy with others. Both the decreased tendency to self-disclose and the disruption in the ability to share intimacy with others have important implications for how trauma is treated in a therapeutic context.

Implications for Treatment

A reluctance to self-disclose on the part of trauma survivors may impact their ability to utilize some treatments. For example, traditional talk therapy would have its limits and challenges with survivors who are reluctant to disclose. Expressive writing, which implicitly engages the mind and body, may provide a format that is less shameful or emotionally arousing than face-to-face self-disclosure.

In addition to the possibility that survivors' reluctance to self-disclose and interpersonal difficulties would require pioneering treatment approaches, the biological underpinnings of trauma point to the need for broader, more innovative treatments for traumatic stress as well. The chronic over-arousal of traumatic stress that leads to emotional over-engagement or under-engagement necessitates a flexible treatment that can facilitate emotional regulation among clients. Impairments in emotional regulation that go hand-in-hand with handicaps in social relatedness and the ability to foster intimacy leads one to question the expectation that clients be able to engage effectively through traditional talk therapy methods. Future treatment may need ways besides one-to-one discourse to teach the client to self-reflect, as well as to express and identify one's own emotions. Lastly, disruptions in representational memory, and the ability to understand the larger context in which a particular event occurs points to the need to create meaning and construct a narrative of traumatic memories.

Along with cognitive, interpersonal, and biological factors, the symptom picture of complex trauma indicates the need for a comprehensive and holistic treatment for clients suffering from this chronic type of posttraumatic stress. Herman (1992) and van der Kolk and Courtois (2005) have described how failure to recognize this complex adaptation to trauma is a hindrance to effective treatment for trauma survivors. Herman also posited that effective treatment delivery is often blocked because the connection between current symptoms and past trauma is missed. It seems that this would be the case most often when the presenting disorder is not obviously trauma-related, and the treatment does not take into account the relevance of the trauma in the symptom presentation and does not assume a trauma-sensitive approach. If the underlying issues of trauma are not noticed and addressed, treatment often becomes fragmented and ineffective.

For instance, such fragmented treatment could involve interventions for "co-morbid" conditions that may be irrelevant for individuals with PTSD or DESNOS (van der Kolk & Courtois, 2005; van der Kolk et al., 2005). For trauma survivors, van der Kolk and colleagues (2005) call into question how well treatment manuals fit co-morbid conditions such as anxiety and substance abuse because of the paucity of evidence that standard treatment manuals for co-morbid disorders are applicable to those with PTSD. Van der Kolk and colleagues further suggested that the full range of how one reacts to traumatization should be considered, instead of the current preoccupation with the narrow band of PTSD symptoms currently found in the DSM. They argued that clinicians should understand that trauma reactions may include disturbances in perception, information processing, affect regulation, and impulse control, as well as a negative impact on personality development (van der Kolk et al., 2005).

Ford, Courtois, Steele, van der Hart, and Nijenhuis (2005) proposed that trauma treatment should occur in phases: (a) symptom reduction and stabilization, (b) processing of traumatic memories and emotions, and (c) rehabilitation and life integration after processing trauma. According to Streeck-Fischer and van der Kolk (2000), treatment should also address issues of safety and the "mastery" of trauma-related experiences through words or physical play. To summarize, specialists and researchers in the treatment of trauma's effects suggest an individualized and integrative approach based on the cognitive, behavioral, and biological sequelae of trauma, especially for clients with complex or chronic presentations.

Part II
Current Treatments for Trauma

Many treatments are currently available to alleviate the deleterious effects of trauma. These include cognitive-behavioral therapies, body work or mind-body approaches, psychodynamic approaches, and narrative approaches. There are considerable commonalities among the theories that inform the treatment of trauma, as well as among the techniques used to implement treatment. We will briefly review these approaches, along with the basic elements of each. This will help create a foundation for the understanding of current and future trauma treatment. It is our opinion that future treatment for trauma will involve a synthesis and innovation of different elements used in existing approaches.

As will be shown in Table 2.1 below, there is considerable overlap among approaches to treating trauma. The following domains are addressed: physical awareness; regulation of affect; focus on past, present, and future relative to PTSD; spontaneous recall of trauma memories; exposure to traumatic material; and reinterpretation of beliefs. These various domains are either emphasized or not emphasized in treatment. The overlap is found when one considers whether different elements are accessed either directly or indirectly by treatment. When one considers how explicit and to what degree domains are emphasized, it is possible to see the commonality among the various trauma treatments present today. Specifics of how the treatments overlap and differ will be discussed.

Table 2.1 Global Approaches for PTSD Treatment

Type of therapy	Physical self-awareness	Regulation of affect	Focus on past, present, and future relative to PTSD	Spontaneous recall by type (imagery, narration, written)	Type of exposure (intensity, duration, frequency)	Reinterpretation and creation of new beliefs
Psycho-physiological approaches						
Biofeedback/Neurofeedback - Boudewyns & Hyer (1990) - Davidson, Stein, Shalev, Yehuda (2004) - Peniston & Kulkosky (1991)	Large focus on physical self-awareness. Feedback given to train individuals to physiologically stay in an optimal level of arousal.	Regulation of affect is a large component of this approach and is achieved through modulating one's physical stress response.	Focus is on past traumatic memories and/or currently presented trauma stimuli while assessing physiological arousal in the present.	No explicit spontaneous recall of trauma.	Emphasis is on training clients to induce a neurological state associated with relaxation and sleep. Exposure not an explicit component.	No explicit emphasis.
Bodywork - Curran (2010) - Rothschild (2000) - van der Kolk (2002) - van der Kolk & Fisler (1994)	The body is seen as an integral part to treatment. Physical self-awareness is emphasized with the goal of increased tolerance of trauma-related sensory stimuli and increased experience of efficacy and purpose.	Emotional reactions to traumatic reminders are abolished *experientially*. Affect and dissociation is regulated through engagement of the body.	Focus is primarily on past and present.	Trauma is recalled through focus on bodily movements and through play therapy.	Exposure can range in intensity, frequency, and duration. It is often largely client-directed.	New beliefs and meaning attributed to trauma are explored through therapeutic experience, as well as increased sense of mastery and control.

Type of therapy	Physical self-awareness	Regulation of affect	Focus on past, present, and future relative to PTSD	Spontaneous recall by type (imagery, narration, written)	Type of exposure (intensity, duration, frequency)	Reinterpretation and creation of new beliefs
Psycho-physiological approaches continued							
Pharmacotherapy - Davidson, Rothbaum, van der Kolk, Sikes, & Farfel (2001) - Marshall, Beebe, Oldham, & Zaninelli (2001)	The side effects of medication and reduction of physical symptoms are monitored, usually based on client self-report.	Affect is regulated through the use of psychiatric medications—SSRI's in particular.	Focus is on reducing a broad range of PTSD symptoms (e.g, disrupted sleep, appetite, mood) in the present with medicine—SSRI's, SNRI's, and atypical antipsychotics.	None.	None.	None.
Cognitive-behavioral therapy (CBT) approaches							
Cognitive Processing Therapy (CPT) - Monson et al. (2006) - Resick & Schnicke (1993)	Not explicitly emphasized, but anxiety is monitored during exposure.	Emotion related to the trauma is gradually expressed through reading the written account out loud. Emotions that impact quality of life are addressed.	Emphasis is placed on past traumatic event.	Spontaneous recall occurs through writing out narration of trauma.	Exposure is done using a writing technique where client writes a detailed account of the trauma and then reads this aloud to the therapist. There is high intensity exposure, and duration lasts until there is a reduction in anxiety. Frequency determined by session.	Specific beliefs related to trauma (e.g., guilt, second-guessing, self-blame) are targeted.

(Continued)

Type of therapy	Physical self-awareness	Regulation of affect	Focus on past, present, and future relative to PTSD	Spontaneous recall by type (imagery, narration, written)	Type of exposure (intensity, duration, frequency)	Reinterpretation and creation of new beliefs
Cognitive-behavioral therapy (CBT) approaches continued						
Dialectical Behavioral Therapy (DBT) - Linehan (1993) - Mulick, Landes, & Kanter (2005) - Wagner & Linehan (2006)	Attention is drawn to the body and how physical states coincide with emotions. Physical self-awareness incorporated in the development of mindfulness.	Affect regulation is a main focus of treatment. Cognitive and behavioral strategies are employed to build skills in affect regulation.	Focus is mainly on present behaviors that are disruptive to the client's life.	Clinician is directive when addressing trauma-focused material. Recall of trauma-related material is collaboratively undertaken and fits into the context of identified treatment targets.	Imaginal and in vivo exposure is implemented within the context of generalizing skills that were previously learned. Demonstration of behavioral control is necessary before trauma work begins.	Thoughts and meaning attributions shift as the client learns mindfulness and the principle of dialectics.
Exposure Therapy - Cahill, Foa, Hembree, Marshall, & Nacash (2006) - Cook, Schnurr, & Foa (2004) - Foa & Cahill (2002) - Foa & Rothbaum (1998) - Foa, Rothbaum, & Furr (2003) - Schnurr et al. (2007)	Client reports on anxiety levels throughout exposure.	Client discusses feelings related to traumatic event while imagining trauma. Goal is to reduce fear and anxiety through repeated and prolonged exposure to anxiety-producing stimuli.	Focus is on processing feelings associated with past trauma memories and not so much on present or future life circumstances. Far distant past is not the focus—e.g., family of origin memories.	Client spontaneously recalls memories of trauma mentally and verbally.	Imaginal and in vivo, high intensity, repeated until anxiety levels decrease. Client is often tape-recorded and asked to listen to recordings of the trauma narrative between sessions.	Beliefs about the world, the self, others and the future are changed. For example, perception of danger is challenged through imaginal and in vivo exposure.

Type of therapy	Physical self-awareness	Regulation of affect	Focus on past, present, and future relative to PTSD	Spontaneous recall by type (imagery, narration, written)	Type of exposure (intensity, duration, frequency)	Reinterpretation and creation of new beliefs
Cognitive-behavioral therapy (CBT) approaches continued						
Eye-Movement Desensitization and Reprocessing (EMDR) - Shapiro (1995) - Shapiro & Maxfield (2002) - Silver, Rogers, & Russell (2008)	Client's attention is periodically called to physical arousal and asked to report on subjective units of distress (SUDS).	Goal is to regulate affect by using relaxation techniques after recalling traumatic memories.	Focus is on past and present primarily, but can also focus on future.	Spontaneous recall occurs through imagery or imaginal exposure. Client is allowed to let whatever comes to mind after recalling a traumatic memory.	Exposure intensity can be high, client arousal is gauged by therapist throughout. Client maintains awareness of physical sensations that accompany the memory while attending to bilateral stimulation (e.g., tracking the therapist's fingers from left to right across the line of vision).	Client visualizes traumatic memory while associating a positive cognitive statement with the memory (e.g., "I am lovable and worthwhile").
Stress Inoculation Training (SIT) - Meichenbaum (1974)	Physiological response to trauma is attended to in the process of acquiring coping skills to mitigate physical symptoms.	Clients are taught to change their emotional reaction to the trauma or situation.	Emphasis is on present. Psycho-education provided on trauma and related distress.	Spontaneous recall is not the focus. Coping skills are taught to address cognitive, behavioral, and physiological symptoms.	Coping skills are rehearsed through role-playing, imaginal rehearsal, and gradated in-vivo exposure. Intensity is titrated dependent on hierarchy. Duration of exposure lasts until anxiety is reduced and frequency depends on session.	Meaning of the situation is restructured.

(Continued)

Type of therapy	Physical self-awareness	Regulation of affect	Focus on past, present, and future relative to PTSD	Spontaneous recall by type (imagery, narration, written)	Type of exposure (intensity, duration, frequency)	Reinterpretation and creation of new beliefs
			Cognitive-behavioral therapy (CBT) approaches continued			
Systematic Desensitization - Bowen & Lambert (1986) - Frank et al. (1988) - Rothbaum, Meadows, Resick, & Foy (2000)	Client monitors Subjective Units of Distress (SUDs) level and physical experience of anxiety throughout exposure.	Through exposure client is able to extinguish the fear response and thus modulate affect related to the traumatic experience.	Focus is on past and present, and can involve the future.	Spontaneous recall occurs during imaginal exposure when client imagines the feared stimuli. Therefore, recall is semi-structured because it is prompted by a pre-identified feared stimulus on the hierarchy.	Exposure (usually imaginal) paired with relaxation training. Hierarchy of feared stimuli is created and relaxation training is taught and practiced prior to exposure until subjective anxiety decreases. Frequency determined by session.	Exposure allows client to challenge beliefs which were affected or reinforced by the trauma.
			Psychodynamic approaches			
Attachment Therapy - Ainsworth (1979) - Bowlby (1977) - Dieperink, Leskela, Thuras, & Engdahl (2001) - Main & Morgan (1996)	Physical awareness is incorporated into increasing a client's sense of safety and secure attachment with others.	Transference between client and therapist recreates early attachment relationships. Therapist provides secure attachment as a corrective experience to help the client regulate him or herself emotionally.	Focus is mainly on the past and the present.	Spontaneous recall takes place through dialogue between the client and therapist. This free association can also take place through creative mediums between a child and the therapist.	The repetition of trauma that takes place in the therapeutic relationship is processed along with memories of traumatic events that are spontaneously recalled.	Attachment is built between the client and the therapist and/or the child and the caregiver. The client or child then develops constructive attitudes and behaviors (e.g., through play therapy). Beliefs are restructured in the context of this relationship.

Type of therapy	Physical self-awareness	Regulation of affect	Focus on past, present, and future relative to PTSD	Spontaneous recall by type (imagery, narration, written)	Type of exposure (intensity, duration, frequency)	Reinterpretation and creation of new beliefs
Psychodynamic approaches continued						
Brief Dynamic Therapy - Magnavita (2005)	Awareness of body is explicitly encouraged. Attention is drawn to physical posturing and physiological arousal of client.	Uncovering and expression of core emotions leads to affect regulation.	Past, present, and future are discussed.	Memories are spontaneously recalled. Free association occurs with semi-structured guidance from therapist. Client's internal world (thoughts, dreams, and fantasies) is explored through free association.	Exposure occurs through detailed recall of trauma memories. High intensity with goal of maintaining optimal level of anxiety for processing. Frequency and duration determined by sessions.	Beliefs and meaning are altered/recreated by confronting past and patterns of relating.
Hypnotherapy - Lindy (1996)	Not explicitly emphasized, clients focus on the process of physical relaxation while entering a different state of consciousness.	Abreaction and catharsis is encouraged, which then regulates affect.	Emphasis is on discussing past.	Spontaneous recall through verbal and imaginal free association.	Trauma recalled spontaneously under relaxed state of consciousness. Intensity is lowered through hypnosis. Duration is a large part of session with frequency determined by sessions.	Beliefs are restructured and meaning created through uncovering of and exposure to trauma memories.

(Continued)

Type of therapy	Physical self-awareness	Regulation of affect	Focus on past, present, and future relative to PTSD	Spontaneous recall by type (imagery, narration, written)	Type of exposure (intensity, duration, frequency)	Reinterpretation and creation of new beliefs
			Postmodern/constructivist approach			
Narrative Approach - Guterman & Rudes (2005) - Lee (2004) - Neimeyer (1999) - Onyut et al. (2005) - Petersen, Bull, Propst, Dettinger, & Detwiler (2005) - Schauer, Neuner, & Elbert (2005) - Schottenbauer, Arnkoff, Glass, & Gray (2006) - Speedy (2000)	Emotional and sensory memory is integrated within the autobiographical narrative.	Habituation, or decline of fight-or-flight behaviors and emotional responses, can occur as client labels emotions and creates new stories/meaning when recalling past events. Client narrates his or her whole life up to the present with a focus on detailed reports of traumas.	Focus is on past, present, and future dominant stories (culture-influenced narratives) that are informed by trauma-related beliefs.	Tasks and interventions include the use of imagery, narration, and written word (often through letter writing) in order to spontaneously formulate narratives.	Exposure occurs through the recall of trauma memories and how they are incorporated into the client's larger narratives. Intensity is modulated largely by the client's emotional disclosure. Exposure is subtly integrated into the techniques used with no specified duration or frequency.	The identification of *unique outcomes* helps to create new beliefs or new narratives. These unique outcomes are behaviors, thoughts, and feelings that contradict the dominant story. Externalization of the problem and "restorying" (creating preferred stories about the client's life) helps in the reinterpretation process.

Type of therapy	Physical self-awareness	Regulation of affect	Focus on past, present, and future relative to PTSD	Spontaneous recall by type (imagery, narration, written)	Type of exposure (intensity, duration, frequency)	Reinterpretation and creation of new beliefs
Trauma-informed group treatments						
Seeking-Safety - Najavits (2002) - Najavits, Schmitz, Gotthardt, & Weiss (2005) - Najavits, Weiss, Shaw, & Muenz (1998)	Physical awareness is strengthened through the implementation of self-care and identifying trigger signals.	Emphasizes emotional regulation through anxiety management, anger management, and self-care.	Focus is on present and building coping skills. Future is addressed through building better coping skills and healthy supports.	Spontaneous recall is not explicit part of the program.	None.	Beliefs change through cognitive, behavioral, and interpersonal components. Goal is for client to establish community network and to nurture healthy relationships.
Trauma Adaptive Recovery Group Education and Therapy (TARGET) - Ford & Russo (2006) - Ford, Russo, & Mallon (2007)	Psycho-education on biological aspects of trauma and substance use disorders. Client assisted in preparing for and processing internal and external triggers.	Emphasis on emotional modulation to apply to daily life events. Client goal is to recognize triggers and reactionary emotions in response to triggers. Emotion regulation is emphasized to assist the client in the process of telling his or her life story.	Approach is here-and-now focused where self-regulation behaviors are practiced. Client largely directs when and how discussion of past trauma occurs. The future is also focused on as the client works toward achieving identified life goals.	Spontaneous recall is structured through the composition of an auto-biographical narrative as an experiential treatment component.	Repetitive recall of trauma is not thought to be necessary for recovery. Exposure is achieved through writing an auto-biographical narrative. Intensity, duration, and frequency are determined by the client. Skill-building is required before exposure.	Thoughts and behaviors are evaluated in the process of restructuring beliefs. Phase two involves the development of assigning meaning.

(Continued)

Type of therapy	Physical self-awareness	Regulation of affect	Focus on past, present, and future relative to PTSD	Spontaneous recall by type (imagery, narration, written)	Type of exposure (intensity, duration, frequency)	Reinterpretation and creation of new beliefs
Trauma-informed group treatments continued							
Trauma Recovery and Empowerment Model (TREM) - Fallot & Harris (2002)	Bodily awareness incorporated into skill development.	Skill development (e.g., self-soothing) promotes affect regulation and targets avoidance and numbing symptoms of PTSD. Peer support targets feelings of isolation, shame, and guilt.	Focus is mainly on past and present through cognitive restructuring, skill training, psycho-education, peer support, and contained exposure.	Spontaneous recall not as emphasized. Trauma history recall is brief and goal-directed involving attention to specific aspects of the trauma.	Exposure occurs through brief, goal-directed recall of specific aspects of trauma in group setting. Low intensity and direction. Frequency is relegated to group meetings.	Cognitive restructuring is key component and involves reframing negative cognitions about one's self and the world.

Discussion of a Multidimensional Model

One way to analyze the current, existing treatments for traumatic stress is to consider the domains of experience they emphasize and address. When we do so, we can see considerable overlap and some differences regarding the elements in treatment. Consideration of the various similarities and differences will provide the groundwork from which to consider how expressive writing can be used as an integrative treatment for traumatic stress.

Regarding the domain of physical awareness, it is argued that all the approaches noted in Table 2.1 involve increasing physical self-awareness, either directly or indirectly. In some treatments, this increase in physical self-awareness is subtle and not explicitly emphasized—for example, in cognitive processing therapy or hypnotherapy, clients may go through the indirect process of attending to anxious arousal or relaxation, respectively. However, it is important to consider that although an element in treatment may not be explicitly emphasized, that mechanism is still operating.

Another major common factor of the approaches listed in Table 2.1 involves regulating affect through this increased physical awareness, as well as with emotional catharsis and the restructuring of cognitions. Among the treatments considered, the road to improvement is found by accessing traumatic memories and restructuring the negative affect associated with the event(s). When clients expose themselves to traumatic material, they work through anxiety and emotions stimulated by this material. In this way, processing thoughts about the trauma can allow desensitization and habituation to occur. The new affective and behavioral responses to traumatic stimuli extinguish old, maladaptive reactions such as hyper-arousal and avoidance. In addition, the different therapies aim for the integration of unwanted traumatic cognitive associations and for the reduction of thought/behavioral avoidance strategies (Bryant, Moulds, & Guthrie, 2001).

The approaches reviewed here also provide the client varying degrees of "free association" that include spontaneous thoughts and images. Such emphasis on spontaneous activity across treatment approaches suggests that each approach is tapping the mind's natural mechanisms that are in place to process trauma. In addition, this common element points to the usefulness of art therapy and creative free association through writing in the alleviation of PTSD symptoms.

Through exposure to traumatic material and some degree of spontaneous recall, most approaches attempt to help the client achieve integration by reorganizing and reprocessing traumatic associations that have contributed to maladaptive behaviors and beliefs. Furthermore, the different treatments involve creating reinterpretations or new beliefs associated with the traumatic memory, whether this aim is explicitly pursued by the therapist or not. In general, the process of therapy provides the client an avenue in which to experience affective, cognitive, behavioral, and relational restructuring.

Although current treatment approaches have much in common, they have several differences. It seems that increased physical awareness is an operating dynamic in the various treatments, but that an increase in sensory and bodily awareness may not be explicitly emphasized. Of the approaches reviewed here, only EMDR and body work expressly synthesize activity of the body with exposure and cognitive restructuring. In body work, physical engagement of the body is emphasized over verbal communication in the resolution of trauma (van der Kolk, 2002). Body work can involve developing body awareness through mindfulness, body scans, and safe place visualizations to help ground the client through talking about distressing memories (Curran, 2010; Rothschild, 2000). Toning exercises and muscle tensing can also be used to help clients have positive experiences of being in their bodies, as well as participating in boundary exploration exercises using one's body (Curran, 2010; Rothschild, 2000). In addition, only EMDR and body work appear to postulate that the primary means to recovery is the client attending to two stimuli at once—the body and traumatic associations.

Although the treatments in Table 2.1 appear to allow the client to address past, present, and future, few equally focus on all three periods of the client's historical timeline, and each differs in which area of the timeline is emphasized. In addition, many of the treatments differ on whether or not memories are recalled or how they are recalled, as well as the intensity, duration, and frequency of interventions used. Specifically, there is variation regarding the spontaneous recall of trauma, ranging from traumatic memories not being an area of focus to an in-depth emphasis on recalling trauma through mental, verbal, written, and kinesthetic means. Similarly, the degree of exposure to traumatic memories varies among treatments, but most involve some level of exposure whether it is direct or indirect. As was mentioned, most therapies incorporate the dimensions listed (e.g., regulation of affect and creation of new beliefs) but differ on how much they are emphasized and whether or not they appear as structured and explicit parts of treatment. For example, the emphasis on creation of new beliefs differs among approaches but generally seems to be an associated feature of trauma treatment.

Notably, pharmacotherapy does not employ the use of recall, thought reappraisal, or behavioral change (Davidson, Rothbaum, van der Kolk, Sike, & Farfel, 2001). In contrast, cognitive behavioral therapy (CBT) (Beck, 1995; Bryant et al., 2001; Foa, Rothbaum, & Furr, 2003) directly focuses on evaluating distress-causing thoughts, building coping skills, and modifying behaviors compared to other therapies. Additionally, cognitive reappraisal or reinterpretation is an explicit technique within CBT, EMDR, and narrative approaches, while the recollection of distressing memories is the core focus of psychodynamic approaches. EMDR, in particular, seems to explicitly combine recollection of traumatic memory with cognitive restructuring. According to EMDR's Adaptive Information Processing (AIP) model, memories of traumatic events tend to remain frozen as they were experienced and retain elements of distorted thoughts and perceptions (Shapiro & Maxfield, 2002).

Overall, trauma treatment aims to mitigate the negative impact of trauma in at least one domain of human experience, whether it is physical, behavioral, cognitive, emotional, or spiritual. It is hypothesized that expressive writing can uniquely attend to each of these domains in treating trauma. Writing is a modality through which clients can spontaneously recall traumatic memories and incorporate different degrees of free association. Treatment can involve increased physical awareness, affect regulation, and the creation of new beliefs while focusing on the past, present, and future.

Future Treatment: The Case for Including Expressive Writing

It seems that each therapy, while searching for its niche, captures part of the picture on how to recover from trauma. Some differences are stylistic or modality-based—for example, treatment can differ on how much creative expression is incorporated or how much direction the therapist provides in session. Other differences involve the dimension focused upon, such as the physiological level, the cognitive level, the behavioral level, the emotional level, or the spiritual level. Building on the integrative work of the past (Linehan, 1993; Shapiro, 1995; van der Kolk, 2002), trauma treatment continues to move toward integration and common factors, including an emphasis on building the therapeutic relationship (Mulhauser, 2006). "It is a question of finding in every case the right adjustment, the appropriate integration, the synthesis of what *seems* opposed and is instead, *complementary*" (Assagioli, 1967, p. 11). Ideally, future treatment will retain what works and discard what does not; even so, the mixture of different elements that otherwise have not been found to be effective could still produce a potent treatment for certain individuals (Smyth & Pennebaker, 2008).

Techniques and therapy that treat different human dimensions affected by trauma (e.g., body, thought, emotion, and spirit) are often associated with improvements in those respective areas. However, this is not always the case. Therapists run the risk of providing incomplete or ineffective treatment if one dimension is overly emphasized or certain areas are not addressed thoroughly enough. In addition, emphasizing a certain mode of recovery or technique can have deleterious effects when assessment does not take into account client factors that may be contraindications to such treatment.

This therapeutic reality is the main consideration of this section, particularly regarding the issue of exposure in trauma treatment and how expressive writing can provide a unique mode for accommodating some of the hurdles posed by how to best implement this technique in therapy. Indeed, the one dimension of treatment that involves a higher risk of aggravating a post-traumatic condition than others involves the use of exposure. All the treatment approaches discussed involve some element of exposure, with the exception of pharmacotherapy. Although exposure has proven to be an effective treatment for trauma (Cook, Schnurr, & Foa et al., 2004; Foa et al., 2003; Schnurr et al., 2007), therapists still have reservations about using this technique because of risks including re-traumatization, symptom exacerbation, and the possible increase in drop-out rates (Cahill, Foa,

Hembree, Marshall, & Nacash, 2006). Expressive writing may offer a creative solution to this dilemma by offering a treatment sensitive to regulating emotion and providing a contained way to explore trauma memories.

Many in the field have been concerned about the implementation of exposure in treatment and have engaged in an extensive cost-benefit analysis on this issue (Bryant & Harvey, 2000; Foa & Rothbaum, 1998; Jaycox & Foa, 1996, as cited in Foa & Meadows, 1997; Pitman, Altman, Greenwald, & Longpre, 1991; van der Kolk, 2002; van der Kolk, McFarlane, & van der Hart, 1996). Van der Kolk (2002) conjectured that the reason intense exposure is associated with high dropout rates (Ford & Kidd, 1998, as cited in van der Kolk) is due to clients feeling "too overstimulated [and] re-experiencing the trauma without immediate relief" (p. 389). Clearly, there are concerns that PTSD symptoms can be exacerbated due to increased arousal/anxiety associated with exposure therapy (van der Kolk, McFarlane, & van der Hart, 1996). Van der Kolk et al. (1996) stated that heightened arousal during exposure therapy may provoke an avoidant or flight response in the client and manifest in dissociation, disengagement, or dropping out of treatment. Contrary to this position, Foa, Zoellner, Feeny, Hembree, and Alvarez-Conrad (2002) found that *imaginal exposure*, or the repeated recounting of traumatic experiences, was not associated with increased drop-out rates. Clients in their study demonstrated a small increase in general anxiety symptoms after beginning imaginal exposure. However, those who reported initial symptom exacerbation were found to benefit from treatment as much as those who did not report such initial increases in anxiety. Thus, graded exposure approaches seem to be the most helpful.

Additionally, van der Kolk et al. (1996) posit that if habituation does not successfully occur, the client may continue to associate heightened arousal with trauma-related stimuli and therefore, not be able to have a corrective experience. This is certainly a risk if exposure is not correctly tailored to the client. Proper exposure therapy involves the monitoring and continued assessment of self-reported subjective units of distress (SUDs), with the goal of decreased SUDs signaling the process of habituation. In general, it seems that inappropriate exposure can lead to the exacerbation of PTSD symptoms and even decompensation.

Given that exposure may be counter-therapeutic if improperly carried out, it is important to consider how exposure may need to be modified in particular situations and among certain populations. Indeed, it has been noted that there are some cases where prolonged exposure techniques may need to be modified (Jaycox & Foa, 1996, as cited in Foa & Meadows, 1997). One point of view suggests that exposure should not be undertaken when clients are experiencing certain symptoms. Bryant and Harvey (2000) cautioned against the use of exposure techniques early in the grief process, when there are co-morbid disorders such as substance abuse, or when there are ongoing stressors in the client's life. In addition, they suggested that treatment should be solely comprised of cognitive therapy and the addressing of maladaptive interpretations of recalled memories if clients present with catastrophic beliefs (Bryant & Harvey, 2000). This is a limiting position because trauma is so widespread, tends to be complex in presentation, and often co-occurs with other diagnoses. Therefore, exposure treatment is often modified and tailored to the individual client instead of being rigidly implemented.

Evidence for the efficacy of exposure treatment has largely been based on studies addressing the trauma of rape and/or assault in females (Foa et al., 2002; Foa & Rothbaum, 1998). Thus, exposure therapy as the treatment of choice may not be generalizable to other populations. For example, individuals with PTSD who suffer from memories of being a perpetrator may not benefit as much from prolonged exposure (PE) and may even experience a worsening of symptoms (Pitman, Altman, Greenwald, & Longpre, 1991). In their study, Pitman and colleagues found that guilt in veterans was exacerbated by exposure treatment. Foa and Rothbaum suggested that among veterans, it is counter-therapeutic to have repeated exposure to the memories of committing harm toward others. In this case, they recommend treatment using cognitive techniques instead of exposure. Foa and Rothbaum hypothesize that mixed efficacy of exposure among veterans may be due to research involving mostly Vietnam veterans, a group that has been found to be more likely to have participated in war-related atrocities and therefore, generally resistant to treatment.

Another population where exposure techniques may need to be modified is dual-diagnosis clients with PTSD and substance-use disorders (SUD) (Najavits, Schmitz, Gotthardt, & Weiss, 2005). The use of modified exposure in treatment for those with PTSD and SUD was explored via prior research by Coffey, Dansky, and Brady (2003); Coffey, Schumacher, Brimo, and Brady (2005); and Vogelmann-Sine and colleagues (1998). These authors suggested that the use of exposure and EMDR should be used only with individuals who can tolerate and regulate distress, as well as those with minor dissociation, had no traumas before age 15, have no vivid images of traumatic events, and do not have high levels of anger (as cited in Najavits et al., 2005).

In addition, Tarrier and Humphreys (2000), Ehler et al. (1998), and Scott and Stradling (1997) found difficulties implementing exposure therapy among patients with both PTSD and SUD (as cited in Najavits et al., 2005). In their study, Najavits and colleagues (2005) revised exposure therapy for use among men with this dual-diagnosis. Revisions included: (a) clients do not need to focus exclusively on one traumatic incident within an exposure session and can process multiple events; (b) safety parameters are required before treatment and should be implemented throughout (e.g., therapist being on-call, written contract of emergency procedures, voicemail check-ins); (c) the processing of both trauma and SUD memories are encouraged; (d) the client and therapist collaborate on whether, when, and how much exposure is conducted throughout treatment; (e) sessions are shorter (one hour in duration); (f) the therapist's role is emphasized, with therapist acting as "good parent" who explicitly expresses empathy; and (g) methods for overcoming resistance to exposure are emphasized and implemented.

Given the need to tailor exposure treatment to specific trauma populations, guidelines are beneficial in addressing these clinical issues. Elliott, Bjelajac, Fallot, Markoff, and Reed (2005) listed principles on how to effectively provide treatment that reflects "the impact of interpersonal violence and victimization on an individual's life and development" (p. 462). The first principle of trauma-informed treatment is that services must validate and recognize the impact of interpersonal violence on personal development and how an individual copes. This principle is explicitly incorporated in the screening and assessment phase, where the client receives psychoeducation about how PTSD symptoms are a manifestation of the brain engaging in survival mode (Ford, Russo, & Mallon, 2007). This principle is particularly important in considering how a therapist might handle the presentation of previously formed maladaptive coping strategies and is relevant when implementing exposure in treatment. For example, dissociation can be understood as a way a person has survived after trauma. This information is helpful in guiding how treatment can be effectively carried out when a client dissociates, such as grounding the client and refraining from flooding the client with trauma-related stimuli.

Clients provide various clues that signal when it may not be the optimal time to carry out exposure in treatment. Regarding dissociation, Bryant and Harvey (2000) state that dissociation indicates that the therapist should take a supportive approach until the client is better able to use therapy. They add that if exposure can be tolerated by the client, techniques can be modified so that exposure is graded, such as directing a client to imagine a scene that he or she feels emotional about and then switching to the traumatic memory. Other signs that signal it may not be the optimal time for exposure include excessive avoidance, anger as the primary presentation, or the presence of extreme anxiety or depression (Bryant & Harvey, 2000). Anxiety within session can be observed through the outward signs of the client's autonomic nervous system and defense reactions. If the client begins dissociating or exhibits a primitive limbic reaction (e.g., fight, flight, freeze), these are signs that the therapist should decrease the level of exposure intensity in the therapy session (Rothschild, 2000).

Another position taken (Rothschild, 2000) suggested that no trauma memories are off- limits as long as therapists remain attuned to the physiological and psychological arousal levels of clients. This is similar to Briere's (2002) concept of the "therapeutic window" where optimum processing of traumatic material takes place in a psychological space between overwhelming exposure and excessive avoidance. Rothschild listed client symptoms that may indicate over-arousal. She stated that parasympathetic arousal in the client can indicate counterproductive therapeutic abreaction. This counterproductive abreaction may be seen in pale or clammy skin, rapid respiration, or emotional sounds coming mostly when the client inhales (Rothschild, 2000).

Additional principles on how trauma-informed services can most effectively be carried out provide insight on how best to implement exposure in treatment. Elliott et al. (2005) states that trauma-informed services should involve collaboration and reduce pressure for the client to conform to certain treatment demands. This is embodied in the treatment approaches of TARGET (Ford et al., 2007) and Seeking Safety + Exposure-Revised (Najavits et al., 2005). In these treatments, clients are given the option to decline discussing any experience they do not wish to address, and the therapist and client collaborate on how much exposure is implemented over the course of treatment.

Lastly, another principle put forth by Elliott and colleagues (2005) states that the goal of trauma-informed services is to minimize the possibilities of re-traumatization. This is perhaps the key principle when considering the positives and negatives of current exposure treatment. The positive aspects of aforementioned treatments relate to how they promote healing, whereas the negative aspects involve how they do not promote healing, either by failing to engage the client or by increasing the risk of re-traumatization. Elliott and colleagues note that this risk is increased by "invasive or insensitive procedures that may trigger trauma-related symptoms" (p. 468). They also suggest that certain confrontational techniques intended to break down denial may trigger memories of childhood abuse. Conversely, not addressing trauma may reactivate memories of having the trauma denied or dismissed (Elliott et al., 2005).

Additional cautions to undertaking exposure therapy suggest that traumatic memories should be prioritized, with most recent traumas addressed first because they are the most accessible and often the reason for the client coming to treatment (Bryant & Harvey, 2000). Bryant and Harvey also suggested that psychoeducation about the therapy needs to be provided if the client is ambivalent or poorly motivated and that exposure needs to be integrated into the client's culture and value system so that it is congruent with his or her views of recovery. Furthermore, it is important for clients to have medical clearance before engaging in exposure because such approaches may trigger severe physiological fight-or-flight reactions in clients.

Clearly, given the potential dangers and inefficacy of exposure when misused, one needs to tailor treatment to the individual. In general, treatment needs to help modulate clients' emotional charge so that clients can more easily engage in and access the healing benefits of therapy. Again, invoking the idea of the "therapeutic window," interventions should be sufficiently powerful to provide enough exposure but not so demanding that they re-traumatize clients (Briere, 2002). Additionally, clinical presentation must be taken into account, and exposure should be integrated into treatment that involves skill building to help manage distressing affects. This need for integration is further emphasized with the growing awareness of the mind-body connection and the need to address physiological, emotional, cognitive, behavioral, and spiritual correlates of post-traumatic stress in an integrated fashion.

Expressive writing offers a comprehensive medium in which to accomplish a synthesis of the above-named dimensions and to explore trauma-related material in a way that integrates best practice principles as discussed above. The use of expressive writing is already part of some trauma treatments including narrative therapy and TARGET (Ford et al., 2007; Guterman & Rudes, 2005). As each individual responds in his or her own way across all dimensions of human experience (i.e., physiological, emotional, cognitive, behavioral, and spiritual), it would make sense for treatment to be person-centered as opposed to exclusively standardized (Lee & Tracy, 2005, as cited in Ford et al., 2007). For example, the amount of structure in expressive writing can be easily tailored by allowing open-ended prompts to segue into more structured exercises. The structure that can be built into expressive writing exercises then supports the need for graded exposure. In general, expressive writing seems amenable to graded approaches where clients have control over what they put to paper. Expressive writing allows for an idiographic approach because it is largely directed by inherent, individual processes of the client. These characteristics of expressive writing allow for graded exposure, but also assist in providing ways for clients to regulate their own affect so as to avoid over-arousal.

Expressive writing provides a modality that can closely follow best practices when exposing clients to trauma-related material. In addition to facilitating a graded approach, expressive writing can help in affect regulation through exercises directly focused on increasing physiological awareness, which helps in the continued monitoring of arousal that is necessary during exposure. Expressive writing can also be used to help ground clients through writing exercises focused on creating safety (e.g., writing about/fleshing out the description of one's "safe place" that can be visualized as a grounding technique). Furthermore, expressive writing is an excellent framework for exposure because it allows for a collaborative process with the therapist and can be easily tailored to the clients' issues and needs (e.g., working on grief issues before proceeding to exposure).

It is unknown how many people have intuitively used expressive writing, such as journaling, bibliotherapy, or letter-writing when coping with trauma, but it is clear that many veterans have turned to expressive writing on their own (McCabe, 2014). Expressive writing provides the flexibility of written recall that can be used to allow a client to tell his or her personal story, thus creating shifts in memory and emotion regulation—two core domains affected by post-traumatic stress (Ford et al., 2007). Interestingly, the structure of expressive writing is often comprised of a beginning, middle, and end, which mirrors different tenses (i.e., past, present, and future) often found in narrative memory. Constructing a picture of one's life through a creative medium can help the person engage narrative information processing to "increase the range, complexity, and contextualization of the client's recent or distant past events so that there is a greater balance of coexisting (rather than fragmented or compartmentalized) negative and positive elements in the recollection" (Ford & Russo, 2006, p. 347). This emphasis toward integration can be especially useful for individuals with complex histories of multiple or prolonged traumas.

Expressive writing, similar to current treatments (e.g., narrative therapy, TARGET), can also mirror the activities used by those who are particularly resilient after a traumatic event. Connecting with others in meaningful activity, participating in rituals, creating symbolic meaning about positive aspects of surviving the experience, reflecting on core human themes (e.g., life and death), and expressing these themes in unique, personal ways (Petersen, Bull, Propst, Dettinger, & Detwiler, 2005) are all a part of expressive writing approaches.

In the next section we will further explore expressive writing as a general therapy technique. In addition, we will discuss how expressive writing has been used in combination with other treatments and how writing has been found to be beneficial to clients, particularly regarding health correlates. Lastly, we will specifically examine meaning-making and expressive writing in the treatment of trauma and the value this may have for clients.

Expressive Writing as a Therapy Technique

> For within living structures defined by profit, by linear power, by institutional dehumanization, our feelings were not meant to survive.
> Lorde, 1984, p. 36, as cited in Maeve, 2000

Art and healing have been deeply associated for millennia (Rojcewicz, 1999). Throughout history, the written word in particular was seen to have special power. For example, the history of poetry therapy can be traced back to religious rites where shamans and witch doctors would use poetic incantations to promote healing (Rojcewicz, 1999). Ancient Egyptians were known to write healing words on papyrus, which were then ingested by the sick to recover from illness. Within contemporary medicine and some psychotherapy approaches, creativity and artistic expression seem to have been greatly de-emphasized. Whereas this is not surprising given the modern Western allegiance to positivistic science and modes of thinking, it is nonetheless interesting given that art and creative expression are linked with human thought, emotions, and spirit, as well as with the development of the self (Harrower, 1972). Indeed, some have argued that medicine and psychotherapy are becoming increasingly based on a scientific "medical model" that is divorced from actual human experience (Miller & Hubble, 2004). Instead, the individual is conceptualized primarily by the symptoms he or she experiences. As a corrective, one of the current goals in medicine and psychotherapy could be the integration of art and human creative expression into the healing process. Already certain theoretical schools of thought such as humanistic, psychodynamic, and narrative therapy emphasize the individual's selfhood in a holistic manner and tend to explore the use of art in therapy more than other approaches (e.g., behavioral therapies). Expressive writing could be a creative way to bridge the gap between these schools of thought and highlight the strengths each has to offer.

Emotional expression has been found to be an excellent healing mechanism and has positive effects on physical and mental health (Kalay, Vaida, Borla, & Opre, 2008; Pennebaker, 1992 as cited in Mazza, 1999). Furthermore, it seems that openly sharing one's trauma has important health implications. Pennebaker and Susman (1988) observed that individuals who did not tell someone about past trauma had 40 percent more visits to physicians than those who had discussed traumas with others (as cited in Pennebaker, 2004). Lamb (2003), in his collected works with the women of York Correctional Institution, wrote:

> Because incest and domestic violence cut across the economic divide, women of all means are schooled in silence. Of the eleven contributors to this volume, eight have been battered and nine have been sexually abused, a statistic that reflects the norm for incarcerated women. Their essays, then, are victories against voicelessness—miracles in print. (p. 9)

Therefore, it seems beneficial for the physical and emotional health of trauma survivors to be able to tell their story. Artistic expression can help clients explore and construct a narrative around past trauma, and ultimately, to aid in the process of discussing and verbalizing trauma.

Art can be one of the most effective ways to encourage emotional expression. It would make sense, therefore, for modern healing approaches to move toward intervention modes that encourage emotional expression through artistic expression. Art could once again be integrated into healing approaches within the fields of medicine and psychotherapy. The use of artistic expression may be particularly helpful in aiding those who have experienced trauma. One expressive therapy that has been used with success is bibliotherapy, which involves the therapeutic use of literature, such as being read to or reading (McArdle & Byrt, 2001). As an approach to psychotherapy, bibliotherapy can include expressive writing, which has been defined as "the use of writing to enable people with mental health problems to enjoy and express themselves, develop creativity and empowerment, affirm identity and give voice to views and experiences" (McArdle & Byrt, p. 517). Another term that has often been used interchangeably with bibliotherapy and expressive writing is poetry therapy. Gorelick (2005) and Lerner (1991) described poetry therapy as using the written and spoken word within the therapeutic experience. In poetry therapy, the focus is always on the person, whereas in poetry workshops the focus is on the poem itself (Lerner, 1997). Poetry therapy can involve clients reading poetry that fits with their presenting problems and/or affect states, as well as clients writing creatively to heal (Mazza, 1999). For example, Mazza (1999) has used the reading and writing of poems in couples/family therapy, group therapy, and work with children/adolescents and the elderly. Goals of both poetry therapy and bibliotherapy include promoting change and adaptive functioning, problem solving, participants' self-understanding and accuracy in self-perception, and finding new meaning through novel ideas and information (Rojcewicz, 1999). The objectives of bibliotherapy, expressive writing, and poetry therapy are also congruent with those of psychotherapy on a broader scale. One can see the aforementioned goals echoed in the therapeutic approaches discussed earlier (Corsini & Wedding, 2008).

Therefore, it is easy to see how poetry therapy and the written and spoken word have made their way into different psychotherapeutic contexts. Poetry therapy has been used across populations with various mental health needs, including individuals with severe mental illness such as schizophrenia (Edgar, Hazley, & Levit, 1969, as cited in Mazza, 1999; Tamura, 2001). Gorelick (2005) detailed how the therapeutic use of poetry has also been applied from the perspective of many different theoretical models. For example, Furman (2003) has applied poetry therapy within existentially oriented psychotherapeutic practice. Here, he assisted clients in exploring their experience and finding life's meaning through the use of poetry.

Salutary Effects of Writing

Emotional expression through creative writing is shown to have positive effects on physical and mental health (Kalay et al., 2008; Pennebaker, 1992 as cited in Mazza, 1999). Pennebaker and Seagal (1999) found that engaging in emotionally expressive writing about important personal experiences has positive physical and mental benefits. They suggested that these outcomes stem from individuals forming a story or narrative about their experiences. Pennebaker and Seagal found that those who benefited most from writing tended to use many positive-emotion words (e.g., happy, laugh), a moderate amount of negative-emotion words (e.g., sad, angry), and an increase in the use of insight (e.g., understand, realize) and causal words (e.g., because, reason). Additionally, Pennebaker, Hughes, and O'Heeron (1987) observed lower physiological indicators of stress (i.e., blood pressure and heart rate) among individuals who had just written about emotional topics. Benefits of expressive writing also seem to extend to mental health where Lepore (1997) found improved long-term mood after expressive writing (as cited in Pennebaker, 2004).

More specifically, expressive writing has been used to attenuate the effects of trauma in many populations. These include those affected by terrorist attacks (Fernandez & Paez, 2008; Honos-Webb, Sunwolf, Hart, & Scalise, 2006), incarcerated women (Maeve, 2000), rape survivors (Brown & Heimberg, 2001), people living with HIV/AIDS (O'Cleirigh, Ironson,

Fletcher, & Schneiderman, 2008), the bereaved (O'Connor, Nikoletti, Kristjanson, Loh, & Willcock, 2003), those with friendship loss (Furman, 2004), and those who have lost a job (Soper & Von Bergen, 2001). The majority of findings have demonstrated benefits from the act of writing in processing the experience of upsetting and traumatic events.

Burton and King (2008) found that there were health benefits to writing about trauma, even when writing for only two minutes for two days. This suggests that it is unnecessary for writing sessions to be lengthy in order to engage the brain's natural process of reorganizing and integrating emotionally laden memories. Similarly, Smyth and Helm (2003) found that writing about traumatic experiences was associated with reports of better sleep and fewer physical symptoms. Smyth, Hockemeyer, and Tulloch (2008) found that expressive writing greatly attenuated neuroendocrine (cortisol) responses to trauma-related memories. When exposed through imagery to traumatic memories at follow-up, those in the expressive writing group versus the control group showed less of a neuroendocrine stress response and recovered more noticeably than the control group. The increased capacity to regulate physiological arousal seems linked to an increased ability to regulate moods. In their study of people living with HIV/AIDS, O'Cleirigh et al. (2008) found that higher levels of emotional disclosure, and processing of traumatic experiences relates to health and immunological benefits, again suggesting that expressive writing appears to have beneficial effects on physiological responses to traumatic stimuli. In addition, it is possible that confronting traumatic stimuli while engaging the body through writing (via longhand or typing) can serve to ground the client and keep the client from dissociating. A decrease in dissociation is helpful in allowing more depth in emotional processing and therefore, increases the effectiveness of the therapy.

However, not all research has supported the positive physiological outcomes of written emotional disclosure (Kloss & Lisman, 2002). Kloss and Lisman found that physical health outcome measures did not differ in a trauma disclosure writing group, a positive emotion writing group, and a neutral writing group. Health was comparable among these three groups before and after disclosure experiences. Kloss and Lisman speculated that a floor-effect could have occurred because they did not use a clinical or highly stressed population. Considering this overview of research taken as a whole, there is evidence that psychotherapeutic interventions benefit from the addition of expressive-writing techniques.

Increased effectiveness may be partly due to the way writing affects the brain and body, as suggested by research described above. Given the effects of traumatic experience on the central nervous system, traumatic stress would be expected to negatively affect health, and interventions could be sought to re-regulate the central nervous system resulting in better physical and psychological outcomes. Expressive writing could help achieve this by affecting change on a neuronal level and is a relevant mode of treatment given the impact of trauma on the brain. The benefits of writing may partly relate to how it re-engages parts of the brain associated with traumatic re-experiencing and language formation. Rauch et al. (1996, as cited in van der Kolk, 2002) showed that when people relive traumatic experience, there is decreased activation of Broca's area and increased activation of the limbic system in the right hemisphere of the brain. Thus, when people with PTSD relive trauma, they have great difficulty putting their experiences into words. Furthermore, Bruner (2002) found evidence suggesting a neurological link between the inability to tell and/or understand stories (dysnarrativia) and deficits in the development of a sense of selfhood (as cited in Lee, 2004). These findings may be particularly salient in trauma survivors who often experience a disrupted sense of self following traumatic events (Janoff-Bulman, 1989). It appears that it may be necessary for trauma survivors to construct narratives of their experiences, and to engage in linguistic-semantic processing—two goals that can be achieved through expressive writing.

In addition to physical health and biological parameters, expressive writing has been found to have salutary effects on role functioning and psychological well-being (Smyth & Helm, 2003). Pennebaker (2004) cited several studies (Cameron & Nicholls, 1998; Lumley & Provenzano, 2003; Pennebaker, Colder, & Sharp, 1990) demonstrating that students earn higher grades in the semester following a writing study. Pennebaker (2004) speculated that this may be due to an enhancing effect that emotional writing has on working memory, or the ability to mentally hold information temporarily and plan complex tasks. In Smyth and Helm's case study, a woman suffering from PTSD reported feeling more "peaceful" and more optimistic about her future after writing about the most traumatic experiences in her life. In addition, she reported improved moods and reductions in anxiety. Abuse-related intrusions still existed, but she reported that they interfered less in her daily life. Similar evidence for mood improvement after writing about trauma was found among the survivors of the Madrid terrorist attack (Fernandez & Paez, 2008). Specifically, survivors reported fewer negative emotions when writing about their memories of the trauma as well as their thoughts and feelings about the attacks, compared to a control group who wrote about recent social activity (Fernandez & Paez, 2008).

In addition to improvements in mood, expressive writing through the use of journaling has been found to decrease trauma symptoms in general (Honos-Webb et al., 2006). Such improvements in PTSD symptoms were found immediately following the writing intervention. This finding contradicts reports that writing about traumatic experiences increases subjective distress. In addition, storytelling was found to decrease trauma symptoms, particularly among those with prior histories of bereavement.

In the treatment of PTSD, Smyth, Hockemeyer, and Tulloch (2008) also found that expressive writing helped improve mood and contributed to post-traumatic growth (i.e., increased new possibilities, personal strength, and appreciation for life). Similarly, Guastella and Dadds (2006) observed increased reports of positive growth when writing focused on finding benefits resulting from trauma. King and Miner (2000) also found that those who are able to find meaning and possible benefits resulting from tragedies are able to cope better than people who find no benefit (as cited in Pennebaker, 2004).

Writing also seems to assist in the process of meaning-making, in addition to improving physical and emotional symptoms of traumatic stress. Park and Blumberg (2002) addressed the question of whether writing assists in the process of meaning-making and whether or not meaning-making includes a change in situational meaning, global meaning, or both. Writing about trauma changed appraisals of trauma across time, which was associated with less distressing situational meaning. Events were also perceived as less uncontrollable and less threatening, and the trauma was eventually thought of as less central and less currently stressful. Related to lessened appraisals of current stressfulness and uncontrollability were increased resolution/ acceptance, understanding, and congruency in the narratives. In addition, there was a decrease in intrusion and avoidance symptoms. Thus, writing about trauma seems to have protective effects on participants' well-being with associated changes in situational meaning given to traumatic events.

Cognitive Restructuring in Poetry Therapy

Mental health benefits from writing have also been demonstrated in studies combining writing techniques with cognitive therapy (Guastella & Dadds, 2006; Kalay, Vaida, Borla, & Opre, 2008; van Emmerik, Kamphuis, & Emmelkamp, 2008). To date, there has been minimal exploration of the application of poetry therapy within major psychotherapeutic approaches, even though many orientations have a rich background of incorporating bibliotherapy (Wright, Basco, & Thase, 2006). Clients might be asked to read manuals or self-relevant biographies about their disorders to gain knowledge and to guide their therapeutic process. In addition, there is a large writing component to approaches such as CBT, which can involve clients actively recording their automatic thoughts and generating rational statements. Such methods have been shown to be effective in cognitive restructuring (Beck, 1995; Corsini & Wedding, 2008; Wright, Basco, & Thase, 2006). Despite the reading and writing components of CBT, as well as other approaches, the incorporation of poetry and creative writing is limited, if not largely absent in practice, from the therapeutic technique "tool boxes" found in many orientations.

Research by Collins, Furman, and Langer (2006), as well as Kalay, Vaida, Borla, and Opre (2008), demonstrates two efforts to combine cognitive therapy with writing exercises. Collins and colleagues (2006) present poetry therapy exercises that are congruent with the goals of cognitive therapy and focus on the client's perceptions of life and his or her beliefs. The creative exercises proposed include: (a) writing a story from the perspective of an irrational belief in order to help the client explore unhelpful beliefs, (b) using Rational Emotive and Behavioral Psychotherapy (REBT) principles by writing a poem in order to exaggerate an irrational belief, and (c) writing a poem from the perspective of a more adaptive belief in order to help clients integrate their new belief. The approach espoused by Kalay and colleagues (2008) included expressive writing enhanced by REBT used by depressed, college-aged women. The group with the REBT writing task had a 10-minute introduction to the principles of REBT followed by a 20-minute session of writing about the most distressing thoughts, feelings, and events participants experienced. The participants were then asked to interpret their writings through the learned REBT principles. Overall, the emphasis appeared to be on teaching REBT principles to the participants along with requiring self-report of irrational beliefs and their rational counterparts. The work of Kalay et al. (2008) seems to lack the deeper integration of cognitive principles within writing tasks evidenced in the work by Collins and colleagues (2006).

As mentioned earlier, creative writing can provide a unique way for clients to reflect on how their thoughts are connected and related to each other. Although distortions in thinking patterns can be pointed out within writing samples, feedback should also incorporate a focus on meaning-making, as well as increased physiological awareness (e.g., through clients attending to physiological arousal when writing). These different components have all been found to be effective in the previously discussed treatments for trauma and can be important components for expressive writing treatment in this area.

Along with cognitive and behavioral components, writing can be used to facilitate emotional processing. In their study, van Emmerik, Kamphuis, and Emmelkamp (2008) compared the efficacy of writing assignments to CBT in treating traumatic symptomatology. Structured Writing Therapy (SWT) consisted of writing in three phases: (a) the first phase involved writing detailed, sensory accounts of the trauma and the emotions felt; (b) the second phase involved writing advice to an imagined someone that had experienced the same trauma on how best to deal with the event and its consequences; participants were also asked to try and apply this advice to themselves; and (c) in the third phase, participants were asked to compose a letter to a person involved in the event that described the event, its impact, and how the participant was coping; in addition, the participant was asked to explain the purpose of the letter, why it was addressed to that particular person, and the reaction (if any) he or she expected to get from the person. All essays were written at home and discussed in treatment sessions. They found that SWT was equally effective as CBT in reducing intrusive symptoms, depression, and state anxiety (van Emmerik et al., 2008). It is possible this equal effectiveness may be partially due to similar mental processes at play in either therapy.

Guastella and Dadds (2006) studied whether writing exercises could be structured to engage cognitive, behavioral, and emotional processes similar to those used in cognitive therapy. These processes include exposure, reappraisal of trauma involving identification and modification of negative beliefs, and benefit-finding. Participants, as well as independent raters assessed the degree to which participants engaged in each of the different cognitive processes (exposure, reappraisal, benefit-finding) based on the writing samples. The writing samples were also analyzed for positive words, negative words, insight words, and causal words. Additionally, participants were asked to rate their subjective distress, and wore a device that monitored their heart rate while writing. Guastella and Dadds (2006) found that intrusive and avoidant symptoms were reduced when writing geared toward exposure was employed. In addition, reports of positive growth increased when writing focused on benefit-finding. These outcomes suggest that writing can be structured in order to engage individuals with specific psychologically related challenges (Guastella & Dadds, 2006).

Writing as a means of cognitive and emotional processing can be a particularly important asset considering the disruption of emotional regulation found in many trauma survivors and other clinical populations. Overall, it appears that when expressive writing is used in treatment to process upsetting events, there is improvement in physical, cognitive, behavioral, and emotional domains of experience.

Distress Induced by Trauma-Focused Writing

Expressive writing may provide a vehicle for clients to emotionally regulate themselves while organizing traumatic memories in a different way than traditional exposure methods. Regarding hyper-arousal or dysregulation, it is important to consider how expressive writing as a treatment for trauma impacts affective arousal and the subjective sense of distress. Regarding distress levels experienced during structured "exposure" writing, Guastella and Dadds (2006) found that with each consecutive writing session, distress decreased. In addition, the exposure writing group did not differ from the standard or reappraisal writing groups in overall reported distress, even though those in the exposure writing group exhibited higher somatic activation through increased experience of body sensations and heart-beat elevations while writing. Such a difference suggests that although exposure-focused writing may initially increase physiological arousal, it may not differ from other writing exercises in regard to subjective experience of distress during and after the exercise.

Nevertheless, writing a narrative of an upsetting or traumatic experience is an intense process for most. Kloss and Lisman (2002) found that state anxiety ratings of college-aged participants indicated that fear increased after each session of writing about their most upsetting experiences and that this did not decrease across the three days of writing sessions. However, it is also possible that these writing sessions (comprised of three, 20-minute sessions in total) did not provide adequate exposure for desensitization. Perhaps a longer period of time for each writing session or across writing sessions is necessary for exposure-informed writing paradigms.

Brewin and Lennard (1999) found that the experience of typing out a stressful experience decreased subjective report of negative affect as opposed to those who wrote long-handed accounts. Although those who wrote long-handed accounts reported greater negative affect, they also reported greater disclosure and perceived benefit. Brewin and Lennard suggested that typing about traumatic memories may be useful for those who find it difficult to tolerate the affect aroused by hand writing. Overall, it seems that the action of typing about distressing topics may relax the client, or create enough emotional distance to achieve the regulation of arousal and increase the effectiveness of the intervention.

Conclusion

Expressive writing for trauma can be thought of as a nuanced and holistic approach to expressing emotion and imagining the events and stimuli associated with trauma (i.e., imaginal exposure). In addition, expressive writing provides a way to uncover core beliefs about the self, world, and others that have been distorted by traumatic experiences (Penn, 2001). By expressively writing about trauma, one expresses emotions, trauma stimuli are imagined, and thoughts surrounding the trauma are reflected upon. A few major benefits are possible: (a) a means for emotional catharsis that can help reorganize brain pathways and improve mood-regulation, memory, and semantic abilities, (b) more accurate uncovering of automatic thoughts and schemas (using clients' personalized language through expressive writing), and (c) a deeper, more comprehensive approach to encountering trauma-associated stimuli through imaginal exposure. Imaginal exposure coupled with expressive writing might appeal to some therapists who believe client stress associated with exposure needs to be buffered. Van Emmerik et al. (2008) suggested that structured writing techniques (involving expressive writing) may be less emotionally demanding than traditional imaginal exposure. They hypothesized that structured writing allows the client greater control over negative emotion that may otherwise lead to dissociative-anxiety, thus allowing for more optimal emotional processing. Similarly, clients may experience both an increased sense of control and personal distance from traumatic events through expressive writing. The client may not have to verbalize written material, which may circumvent any shame or additional emotional distress that would result from discussing trauma.

Rossiter and Brown (1988) found that poetry therapy was particularly beneficial for withdrawn patients, and not as helpful for patients with deficiencies in cognitive functioning (e.g., brain damage, delusions) (as cited in Mazza, 1999). Pennebaker (2004) suggests that guarded, hostile men may particularly benefit from writing because they are the least likely to discuss emotions with others. Mazza (1999) cautioned that poetic techniques may not help the therapeutic process by promoting intellectualization or by bringing up feelings that the clients may not be ready to deal with given their current resources. Regarding this latter topic, Pennebaker (2004) advises that expressive writing may not be beneficial for those who have recently experienced trauma (e.g., in the last few days or weeks) due to trauma-related disorientation and distress. He also advises that clients refrain from writing if they feel that they will become too emotionally distressed by writing about a particular topic. These issues must be taken into account and monitored throughout treatment.

Further support for creative writing is that the act of writing expressively may engage different parts of the brain not accessed by verbal narrative, or mentally recalling the details of the memory. Williams (1992) assessed the belief systems of adult survivors of childhood sexual abuse through the administration of the Williams-McPearl Belief Scale (measuring beliefs about safety, trust, power, self-esteem, and intimacy) along with poetry and journal entries of the survivors (as cited in Mazza, 1999). Williams (1992, p. 19) stated that "the creative writing of survivors of sexual abuse reveals much otherwise hidden or repressed information about their abuses, self-concepts, and basic beliefs" (as cited in Mazza, 1999). It seems that the act of writing expressively about trauma may not only provide a unique exposure opportunity (perhaps increased exposure potency), but simultaneously reveal more covert distorted beliefs.

Finally, the act of writing is a creative, generative, and linguistic process that seems to oppose underlying fears of death and dissolution brought about by trauma. Stolorow (2008, p. 282) explains "Drawing on my own experience of traumatized states, I propose that it is the process through which the emotional experience comes into language that the sense of being is born, and that the aborting of this process brings a loss of the sense of being." Similarly, Bunting and Hayes (2008) comment, "Language makes the human achievements of technology and artistry possible, yet this same language allows us to lose touch with experiencing our very existence" (p. 233). Therefore, language can promote a sense of being, and of generativity to counteract the feelings of dissolution caused by encounters with trauma. To conclude, Rollo May (1975) eloquently states, "By the creative act ... we are able to reach beyond our own death. This is why creativity is so important, and why we need to confront the problem of the relationship between creativity and death" (as cited in Schneider, 2008, p. 20).

To capitalize on the unique benefits expressive writing seems to offer, the following workbook is provided to accompany treatment with those who are suffering from traumatic stress. Like treatments that build upon a stage approach (Ford & Russo, 2006; Linehan, 1993), this workbook stresses the primary establishment of safety and healthy coping skills before confrontation with trauma-related material. The first part provides general writing guidelines on how to structure expressive writing therapy sessions to maximize safety, work with client resistance, and manage emotional dysregulation. The workbook then is partitioned into beginning, intermediate, and advanced exercises including different types of writing exercises graded by amount of pacing and structure. Skills targeted within these sections involve building rapport, safety, and physical and emotional awareness. The remaining two parts with exercises include free-writing exercises and activity-based exercises. Clients are guided from focusing on the past and resolving grief, toward the present to articulate current problem areas, and finally to the future to engender hope and goals. Traumatic memories and associations are recalled in an effort to create a personalized, integrated narrative. While clients' sense of self and meaning change, they attend to their related thoughts, emotions, and physical sensations. The workbook concludes with suggested outcome measurements that can be given prior to, during, and after treatment to assess change. Areas of measurement include posttraumatic symptomatology and the therapeutic alliance.

Part III
Expressive Writing Workbook

Much of the inspiration for the following workbook comes from the leaders in the field of bibliotherapy (such as Kathleen Adams, Nicholas Mazza, and James Pennebaker). We have often adapted their work to use with post-trauma symptoms. The types of writing exercises that follow in this manual fall along a continuum where individuals start out with more structured, concrete, and informational exercises and progress to more insightful, abstract, and intuition-oriented exercises (Adams, 1998). Similarly, within each section, exercises are organized to progress from safety-focused exercises, to raising awareness of the self, current problems, and important others, to exposure, and then to more insight-oriented work. Clinicians are encouraged to use their judgment about what is needed for clinical work, and when.

General Writing Guidelines

Endeavoring to begin therapeutic writing on one's own can certainly be helpful in some cases, and there are workbooks proposed to aid individuals in this regard (e.g., "self-help" books; Adams, 1998; Pennebaker, 2004). It is argued that although participating in writing activities on one's own can be engaging and healing, collaboration with a therapist is advisable for those dealing with traumatic stress. Issues of traumatic stress often involve emotional regulation difficulties that include both dissociation and emotional deadening on one end and hyperarousal on the other. Both extremes can lead to individuals having difficulty self-motivating and engaging in a solo writing program. Perhaps when symptoms have improved, clients may be able to use and find more benefit with independent expressive writing as proposed by Adams (1998) and Pennebaker (2004). However, collaboration with a therapist is useful in engaging the client in the very act of writing, which can be difficult to undertake for those dealing with traumatic stress.

Additionally, the therapeutic context and relationship provide boundaries within which to grapple with emotionally triggering thoughts and memories. The context of a therapy session provides a very real encounter between people and allows the client to step out of the therapeutic writing mode and enter back into "real" life. This necessary transition back into everyday life has been alluded to by Pennebaker (2004) who advises that there will always be some time for reflection after every writing exercise (Petrie, Booth, & Pennebaker, 1998, as cited in Pennebaker, 2004). For some people, assuming time for reflection on one's own may be beneficial; however, with many posttraumatic stress-complicated disorders it is important to undertake this careful reflection with the aid of a skilled, trauma-informed clinician. Reflection time would be maximized by starting writing exercises toward the beginning of the session so that there is plenty of time for reflection during the remainder of the session. Reflection and verbal processing do not mean that clients are required to share the exact details of their writings—the choice to share actual writing samples should be left to clients in order to protect privacy and encourage a sense of safety within the therapeutic relationship. The time used to reflect on writings seems to be very important in extending any resultant insights or thoughts, and to fortify cognitive and emotional reorganization that may have occurred during the act of expressive writing.

Structuring Client Writing Activities during Session

Pacing and Containment

Pennebaker (2004) suggests that when individuals engage in an expressive writing exercise, they should write continuously for a set period of time (usually 10 to 20 minutes). Adams (1998) also promotes continuous writing within time constraints. This approach is better suited for more open-ended exercises suggested later in this workbook. Even for more structured exercises like sentence completion, clients should be encouraged to write as automatically as possible and not spend time analyzing what they spontaneously write. This can help clients prevent self-censorship and reveal covert or "automatic" thoughts.

Adams (1998) recommends providing pacing and containment through a graded approach to protect clients from jumping into unstructured writing exercises that may flood them with overwhelming feelings regarding any traumatic material that has surfaced. Adams (1998) also suggests a few techniques to help writers build pacing or control rhythm, movement, and timing. First, Adams recommends writing the word "BREATHE" at the top of the page so that writers can see the word and remember to take a breath during their writing session. A second recommendation by Adams is for writers to record a statement of their intentions at the beginning of the writing session so they can go back and review it to make sure they are focused. A third recommendation by Adams that is useful across all exercises is for clients to write three "feeling" words at the beginning and end of every writing session. This activity may help clients become more aware of their internal emotional states, and assist in building skills on communicating affect and mood to others. Lastly, Adams recommends "Bridging Back to the Present" after writing (1998, p. 70). In a similar vein, we suggest the following exercise to help bring the individual back to a present focus:

> What makes you a unique person? Please describe your favorite accomplishments, life roles, or possessions that set you apart from others. When you look around your work place or living space, what are the things that show the world who you are? Do you have a favorite calendar on the wall or a music collection that defines you? Please be as specific as possible in your descriptions.

The chosen object serves as the "bridge" back to the present. It may be helpful to establish such a bridge before starting any of the writing exercises presented here, so that clients can imagine an effective grounding object when needed after an emotional writing experience. The above techniques all help to provide pacing and containment when engaging in therapeutic writing.

In later sections of this workbook, we provide suggestions for using relaxation techniques, imagery and visualization exercises, and multi-media tasks to help clients regulate emotions during exposure to upsetting stimuli. Therapists may wish to read these later sections first and/or use these exercises with clients before starting any type of writing exercise that requires exposure to traumatic stimuli.

Closing the Session

Pennebaker (2004) suggests using post-session follow-up questions to help clients reflect on their writing experiences; they may be a useful way to begin the reflection phase of the session after the client completes one of the writing exercises in this workbook. Such questions lend themselves to some of the writing exercises better than others. The following questionnaire has been created for use after any expressive writing exercise and includes open-ended questions to elicit identification of feelings:

Rate the following items using the 7-point scale given below:

1	2	3	4	5	6	7
None			Somewhat			A great deal

1. I expressed my deepest thoughts and feelings____
2. I currently feel upset____
3. I currently have positive feelings____
4. Today's writing was valuable and meaningful for me____
    Please answer the following questions:
5. What do you like/not like about the writing exercise you just completed?

6 What feelings did you notice?
7 What did you learn about yourself?
8 When might you use this writing technique for other issues that come up?
9 In the space below, briefly describe anything else about how your writing went today:

> **Clinical example:** *For Monica, the use of boundaries in her writing was crucial for therapy. She had anxiety about her ability to delve into certain topics. In order to contain this anxiety, she started the writing exercise in session by taking a few deep breaths and practicing mindfulness and attention to the present. She wrote "BREATHE" at the top of her page, and her writing was timed for 10 minutes to allow for sufficient reflection and processing afterward.*
>
> *Monica, like many trauma survivors, grappled with issues of attention and concentration, occasionally slipping into dissociation. The "BREATHE" at the top of her page, along with the structure of the exercise, helped her to more fully engage in the writing experience in a safe way. Following her writing, she was able to effectively answer the post-writing follow-up questions, helping her to focus on the feelings elicited by the writing, thus enhancing her ability to mentalize, or to reflect on, her thinking and feelings (Fonagy, Gergely, Jurist, & Target, 2002, as cited in van der Hart, Nijenhuis, & Steele, 2006). She then transitioned to writing a few brief sentences in response to the "Bridging Back to the Present" exercise (Adams, 1998, p. 70), serving as a written way to ground herself following her engagement with emotionally charged material.*

The general guidelines laid out above apply to the various types of exercises that will now be described below. Each section will describe a different type of writing exercise, from highly structured and paced exercises, to less structured and free-writing exercises. Again, clinicians should use their own judgment about where to begin and which exercises are most relevant to the needs of the individual client.

Part III-I
Beginning Exercises

Section 1: Lists and Clusters

Word lists (and clusters of related words) act as prompts that promote communication and insight, and may help clients warm up to future free-style writing beyond the simple task of creating written lists. Completing lists and clusters when starting expressive writing may also help clients feel a sense of accomplishment. However, clients with narcissistic traits, or those who want to be perceived as skilled may perceive creating lists/clusters as an affront due to their high level of structure and simplicity. It is important to use clinical judgment when selecting exercises for use in therapy. If a client is offended or has a negative reaction to a particular exercise, it is advisable to fully explore this reaction and what meaning the client made from the experience (e.g., "The therapist doesn't think I'm smart or doesn't want to talk about what really matters to me"). Then the therapist has more information for selecting future exercises that fit better with clients' personality styles and clinical needs.

Why Begin with Lists and Clusters?

In early recovery from post-traumatic stress, containment through cognitive-focused strategies may be the preferred treatment strategy as opposed to exploration of clients' trauma history (Herman, 1992; Kaufman, 1989, as cited in Najavits, 2002; Najavits et al., 1998). A sense of safety can be encouraged by engaging the client in simple and relatively neutral writing activities (e.g., generating lists and clusters of words) and then moving to more free-style writing exercises (e.g., sentence stems, then poems, and so on) in order to alleviate frozenness or hyperarousal (Streeck-Fischer & van der Kolk, 2000); word list/cluster exercises seem to meet these criteria. Exercises in this section may also help clients deal with resistance to writing techniques in general.

The focus at this stage is on engaging in simple therapeutic writing activities and building coping resources. Emotional dysregulation, dissociation, and interpersonal problems should be attended to before processing specific traumatic memories, even in written form (van der Kolk et al., 2005). In addition, it is imperative to begin therapy with "establishing … positive rapport between the therapist and the patient" (Assagioli, 2000, p. 88, as cited in Firman & Gila, 2010). Exercises geared toward building the relationship with the therapist can also be introduced, since research exploring common factors shows that a key element among therapies is the quality of the therapeutic relationship (Mulhauser, 2006). Creating word lists and clusters of related words may serve to help build rapport early in the relationship.

In the primary stage of safety and coping, exercises will focus on teaching the client how to cope with challenging or distressing affect while building trust with the therapist. As shown below, general writing exercises are introduced first, which allow clients to become comfortable with this modality in session. Careful selection of exercises in this section draw clients' attention to the moment, and engaging in these activities can serve to increase cognitive and emotional awareness.

Increased self-monitoring and a sense of self-control can be achieved by teaching emotional awareness in the later word list/cluster exercises. Clients will learn how to name and tolerate sensations, feelings, and experiences. Mazza (1999) states that by writing about personal feelings, clients begin to identify their feelings more coherently and gain a sense of control. These types of exercises can also provide a gateway to discussing the client's life and potential problems, as well as a way for the therapist to enter a client's "life space" (Mazza, 1979, as cited in Mazza, 1999).

The goal is for clients to "own" what they feel before moving on to explicitly trauma-focused material. In avoidant individuals, emphasis can be placed on feelings, while emphasis may be placed on thoughts for ambivalent individuals (Streeck-Fischer & van der Kolk, 2000). When distressing affect arises, efforts will be made to record associated thoughts that can be re-evaluated later. This section on creating word lists and clusters moves from simple activities meant to help clients become comfortable with basic writing tasks, to more complicated activities that require clients to engage in direct exposure to internal states (thoughts, feelings, bodily sensations, and so on), and then engage with people and events within their environment (including traumatic experiences).

Lists

In general, clients are expected to list at least five items for each topic or question below, with 10 or so being the ideal range. The length of each list may be revised, based on client preference and type of task. Clients should take no more than five to 10 minutes to create lists for each exercise.

Lists about the Process

Exercise 1: Lists about Lists. This beginning exercise is meant to serve as an introduction to creating lists, and to elicit client opinion about the task itself. This usually only takes a few minutes and requires clients to make a list of the top five positive and negative things about making lists. It is also intended to introduce a small amount of humor into the writing exercise in that the relative irony and absurdity of "making a list about lists" can be shared between therapist and client.

Exercise 2: Lists about therapy. Making a list about the 10 things that clients believe about the therapy process itself can help the client gain further practice with making lists, while also providing information about client expectations relative to therapy. This usually only takes a few minutes, and can help the therapist and client then discuss such expectations and correct misconceptions as needed.

Lists about Personal Positives

Exercise 3: Lists about Personal Strengths and Coping. Clients will generate about 10 things they believe are their greatest strengths and assets, things they've noticed have helped them most throughout their lives. Providing a list of positive attributes early on (before focusing on more negative issues) can serve as a touchstone during later times when distressing feelings and thoughts are directly addressed.

Exercise 4: Things I've Accomplished. Clients list the top 10 things they've accomplished so far in their lifetimes (Adams, 1998). Once again, focusing on positives can help set the stage for dealing with negatives in the near future.

Feeling Lists

Exercise 5: Identifying feelings. Clients are provided with a list of various feelings, with the table below as an example (Wisconsin Relationship Education, 2010). From this list (or another list of the therapist's choosing), clients are to take about five minutes to write down their current top 10 positive feelings, and their current top 10 negative feelings on a separate piece of paper. The purpose of this exercise is to introduce clients to labels that most accurately reflect their current feeling states, as well as to provide exposure to basic writing exercises that are feeling-oriented.

Joyful	Tenderness	Helpless	Defeated	Rageful
Cheerful	Sympathy	Powerless	Bored	Outraged
Content	Adoration	Dreading	Rejected	Hostile
Proud	Fondness	Distrusting	Disillusioned	Bitter

(Continued)

Satisfied	Receptive	Suspicious	Inferior	Hateful
Excited	Interested	Cautious	Confused	Scornful
Amused	Delighted	Disturbed	Grief-stricken	Spiteful
	Shocked	Overwhelmed	Helpless	Vengeful
Enthusiastic	Exhilarated	Uncomfortable	Isolated	Disliked
Optimistic	Dismayed	Guilty	Numb	Resentful
Elated	Amazed	Hurt	Regretful	Trusting
Delighted	Confused	Lonely	Ambivalent	Alienated
Calm	Stunned	Melancholy	Exhausted	Bitter
Relaxed	Interested	Depressed	Insecure	Insulted
Relieved	Intrigued	Hopeless	Disgusted	Indifferent
Hopeful	Absorbed	Sad	Pity	
Pleased	Curious	Guilty	Revulsion	
Confident	Anticipating	Hurt	Contempt	
Brave	Eager	Lonely	Weary	
Comfortable	Hesitant	Regretful	Bored	
Safe	Fearful	Depressed	Preoccupied	
Happy	Anxious	Hopeless	Angry	
Love	Worried	Sorrow	Jealous	
Lust	Scared	Uncertain	Envious	
Aroused	Insecure	Anguished	Annoyed	
Tender	Rejected	Disappointed		
Compassionate	Horrified	Self-conscious	Irritated	
Caring	Alarmed	Shamed	Aggravated	
Infatuated	Shocked	Embarrassed	Restless	
Concern	Panicked	Humiliated	Grumpy	
Trust	Afraid	Disgraced	Awkward	
Liking	Nervous	Uncomfortable	Exasperated	
Attraction	Disoriented	Neglected	Frustrated	

Exercise 6: Creating Metaphors for Emotions. Once clients have become familiar with common emotional descriptors, they are then asked to create a list of metaphors for each of their strongest emotions. For example, a client may list the top five positive emotions as brave, eager, calm, strong, and hopeful. For each of the top five emotions, clients are then asked to create two or three symbols that best represent each of the emotions. To help with this exercise, clients may be asked to take a deep breath, close their eyes, and imagine feeling one of the emotions on the list in order to see what images appear. Clients then note them on a separate page.

Each emotion can have its own page or record with various attributes. For example, clients can be asked to think about what each emotion would be if it was embodied as a type of weather, building, food, song, or action. Clients may also engage the senses by imagining what it would be like if they could see it as a color, sound, taste, or smell. The possibilities are without limit, and you can imagine other metaphors as well. An example for a distressing emotion would be: *Uneasy*—fog, color of gray, ear plugs, song from the movie *Jaws*, stone warehouse.

Exercise 7: Identifying Emotional Milestones. Clients list 10 major emotional turning points in their lives, from birth to present (Adams, 1998). These usually consist of births/deaths, educational/employment milestones, weddings/divorces, and so on.

Past, Present, and Future

Exercise 8: Correcting the Past. After creating a list of major life milestones, clients may create a list of all the things they wish they'd said or done differently during one of these times (as a corrective). In addition, accepting and coming to terms with present difficulties often involves acknowledging past injustices. Clients can make a list of grievances, things that made them mad and have carried over to now. To further bring these issues into the present, clients can make a list of things they will no longer tolerate:

Why I'm Mad:
-
-
-

Things I Wish I'd Said or Done:
-
-
-

Things I Will No Longer Tolerate:
-
-
-

Exercise 9: Gratitude and Future Focus. Regarding lost or present loved ones, clients may create lists about what they love best about each person, and why they would like to thank him or her. This can be coupled with a list of things clients would like to accomplish with the rest of their lives, in light of the legacy from loved ones.

Why I Love You:
-
-
-

Thank You For:
-
-
-

How You Have Influenced My Life:
-
-
-

What I Want to Accomplish with My Life as a Result:
-
-
-

Exercise 10: Desires and Action Needed. The following three topic areas may be helpful in identifying problems and future steps toward change:

These Are the Top Three Things I Want to See Happen (or Want to Have):
-
-
-

These Are the Top Three Things that Are Getting in My Way:
-
-
-

These are The Top Three Things I Could Do Right Now to Take a Small Step toward Getting What I Want:
-
-
-

Exercise 11: Lists Based on the Miracle Question. Similar to the exercise above, clients can create a list of concrete behaviors they can enact following completion of the Miracle Question: "If your problem were magically solved, what are the top three things you'd notice?" (de Shazer et al., 2007). This technique originated from Solution-Focused Brief Therapy, a strengths-based approach that serves to assist clients in imagining what their lives would be like if all their pressures and problems were solved. This can be helpful if clients have a difficult time spontaneously coming up with goals for the future. Also, it may be helpful to engage clients in answering this Miracle Question in order to elicit the behaviors needed to solve problems and gain momentum for change. Asking the Miracle Question can be an excellent way to facilitate clients' imagining what they would like to see happen in their lives and delineating concrete actions and steps toward creating the life they want.

> **Clinical example:** *Cameron was an 18-year-old high school senior who had survived a skiing accident where his friend had died. Since the accident, he exhibited symptoms of depression—namely social withdrawal and a lack of motivation. Fairly early in treatment, the therapist posed the Miracle Question and had Cameron list detailed, concrete behaviors that would accompany his improved life. Cameron then agreed to write a list of 10 behaviors that arose from this exercise.*

Clusters

Similar to word lists, word clusters provide structure while breaking down internal barriers to generating ideas about any given topic, especially ones where individuals feel "stuck" or when emotions are high. Adams (1998, p. 27) provided a nice set of instructions that can help a client get started:

> Write [a word or phrase as a topic] in the center of the page and circle it. What's the first word or phrase that comes to mind? Write this above, below, or to the side of your first word, circle it, and draw a line connecting it to the middle. What does the second word make you think of? Write it down, circle it, connect it with a line to the word before it. Continue in this way until you can go no further [or the page is covered].

Once this process is completed, the client can return to the original word circled in the center of the page, and generate yet another cluster of related words/phrases until nothing more comes to mind. For each cluster exercise, we recommend spending no more than 10 minutes to generate one complete page.

Therapy and Desired Outcomes

Exercise 1: Therapy. Clusters are completed using the word "therapy" or "therapist/therapist's name" as the beginning word/phrase in the center of the page. This helps elicit spontaneous words, descriptors, thoughts, and feelings about therapy in general.

Exercise 2: Main Problems. Clients identify the main problem(s) they are facing (e.g., PTSD, depression) and complete at least one word cluster exercise for each. This helps clients identify further issues around their challenges and to delve more deeply into how they define each problem.

Exercise 3: Goals for Treatment. Clients pick a particular goal (e.g., "dealing with the trauma") and create at least one word cluster in relation to it. This may help identify potential roadblocks, motivational issues, or positive factors that will help them attain their goals.

> **Clinical example:** *Ever since being sexually assaulted, Amber was having a difficult time concentrating at work. When not at work, she would often retreat to her apartment and "zone out" while watching movies and smoking marijuana. She was falling behind in her work responsibilities, and she didn't feel much motivation for anything, which was further exacerbated by her marijuana use.*
>
> *Amber came to therapy after her supervisor at work expressed concern about her performance. She was unsure what she wanted to work on in therapy, and appeared to have limited insight into what was fueling her recent decline in functioning. Therapy also began to take on a hazy quality as Amber's motivational and attentional issues began to influence the therapeutic process. When Amber was guided to complete clusters about her goals, treatment had felt derailed by a lack of focus. It was important for the therapist to address her use of marijuana to help improve Amber's cognitive symptoms. However, some of these symptoms were more characteristic of hypoarousal post-trauma (e.g., dissociation, numbing). Amber was guided in a semi-structured way to think spontaneously about what she wanted. Timing was crucial for the intervention and involved the therapist taking advantage of when Amber had a higher level of mental energy and attention in the absence of dissociation, and at a time of day when Amber would have less cannabis in her system (in this case, in the morning).*
>
> *Amber's written clusters revealed an impaired sense of confidence that was impacting her motivation for change. It was revealed that her lack of confidence was compounded by a general sense of ambivalence about her job in general, which had shifted after the assault. After she had suffered injury to her body, she had a hard time finding meaning in the "daily grind," and following through with work responsibilities. This brief exercise also showed Amber that she was having significant biological disturbances that could be aims of treatment. Primarily, her sleep was being disrupted, and this was impacting her energy levels and motivation.*
>
> *Being able to articulate concrete steps toward her personal goals through further use of this writing exercise, Amber reported an increased sense of direction and agency. Her self-defined goals then directed treatment. Any ambivalence and feelings about these goals were explored in light of her trauma history. She was able to better understand how and why her confidence, motivation, and relationship to her job had changed following the sexual assault, and she was able to take steps to deal with these issues.*

Exercise 4: Desired Personal Quality. Clients identify a personal quality (e.g., patience, perseverance) they would like to acquire and create a word cluster related to it (Adams, 1998). Such an exercise helps generate discussion about possible personality change, over and above problem solving relative to future goals.

Exercise 5: Hope. A cluster may be generated using the topic of "hope," circled at the center of the page. Generating word clusters on this topic may assist clients in identifying their hopes for the future, as well as any potential roadblocks that could get in their way.

Focus on Self

Exercise 6: My Thoughts and Beliefs. Clients create a word cluster that begins with an important thought or belief about the self.

Exercise 7: My Feelings. A word cluster could be generated using a particularly strong emotion (either positive or negative) as a starting point.

Exercise 8: My Body. A cluster may be generated on the topic "my body," centered and circled on the page. A variation of this exercise would focus on a body part that is especially troublesome to the client (e.g., tense shoulders, stomach).

Focus on Important Others

Exercise 9: Family Members. Clients can write word clusters for the topic "family," using the names or role labels (e.g., "mother") of certain family members or intimate partners, centered and circled on the page.

Exercise 10: Other Important People. Clients may also create word clusters using the names or labels of other important people in their lives, such as a best friend, co-worker or boss, neighbor, doctor, police officer, or anyone else who has had a positive or negative impact on them.

Focus on Trauma

Exercise 11: Grief and Loss. Clients may create a word cluster about the process of grieving and the people and things that were lost traumatically. Variations might include creating a cluster on the topic of "grief," or with the name of a lost object—this could be the name of a person, thing, or an abstraction (e.g., "innocence").

Exercise 12: Trauma. Clients can create a word cluster about their trauma, identified as the central topic (e.g., "rape," "disaster," "robbery"), circled in the middle of the page. Additionally, one may write a word cluster using the name of the perpetrator as the central topic (e.g., "rapist," "robber," "perpetrator").

Exercise 13: Guilt, Shame, or Forgiveness. Clusters are generated for the topics "guilt," "shame," and/or "forgiveness." Clients may be provided with the following brief definitions for these words, particularly as "guilt" and "shame" may be confused. Guilt can be thought of as remorse or regret for an action/feeling or inaction that one has deemed immoral. Shame is a feeling of embarrassment or disgrace for something or an action associated with oneself. Forgiveness is not condoning someone's actions or wrongdoing, but extending mercy and/or ending resentment or anger toward the person. It often involves the aim of re-establishing peace in the client's current life.

Section 2: Sentence Stems

Similar to creating written word lists and clusters, sentence stems are semi-structured prompts that promote communication and insight and may help clients warm up to free-style writing beyond the simple task of creating lists/clusters. As shown below, general sentence stem writing exercises are introduced first, to allow clients to become comfortable with this task in session. Similar to creating lists, this section on sentence stems moves from simple activities meant to help clients become comfortable with basic writing tasks, to more complicated activities that require clients to engage in more direct exposure to internal states (thoughts, feelings, bodily sensations, and so on), and then engaging with people and events within their environment (including traumatic experiences).

Defining Who I Am

Exercise 1: Setting the Writer Free. To become comfortable with spontaneous writing tasks in general, clients can complete the following sentence stem as modified from Adams (1998, p. 47):

I can set free the writer [/poet] inside me by …

Exercise 2: Prompts for Imagining a Safe Place. The following exercise assists clients in generating thoughts about when they've felt relaxed and at peace:

Relaxation is …
I feel most relaxed when …
My body doesn't feel tension when …
When I feel calm I …
Safety is …
The place I feel safest is …

The place I find peace is …
The place where I can truly be myself is …

> **Clinical example:** *Barbara and her therapist thought it would be an effective strategy for her to imagine her safe place. This tool would help Barbara with her intrusive post-traumatic symptomatology. She was to increase awareness of triggers and physiological sensations of anxiety so that she could learn how best to practice quiet meditation in her safe place when she was going about her daily life. Barbara didn't have much confidence in her writing abilities, but she felt capable of tackling the "prompts for imagining a safe place."*
>
> *Through spontaneous, quick responses, Barbara was able to easily identify her grandmother's cabin as her "safe place." This would help her later engage in guided imagery about this place. When identifying further details about her safe place, she was able to think about taking a bubble bath there, humming to herself, or walking around the yard, looking out at the lake. Information obtained from Barbara's sentence stems also revealed a deep sense of anxiety and lack of safety that served as important clinical information and material for further therapeutic discussion.*

Exercise 3: Jump-start Writing about the Self. For some clients, it may be a challenge to complete writing exercises that focus solely on the self. The following sentence stems are from "Structured Writing Exercises" proposed by Adams (1998, p. 23), and are used here to introduce self-focus in a general way in order to assist individuals to become comfortable with such tasks:

The first thing that comes to mind …
What feels uncomfortable or disturbs me about this is …
What gives me hope or inspires me about this is …
I would benefit from …
My next step is to …

Exercise 4: Window into self. This exercise is meant to directly focus on self. These sentence stems may clarify how clients feel and think about themselves in general, as well as identify negative cognitions related to trauma. Examples of sentence stems in this arena include: "If you knew me …," "I feel loved when …," "I feel closest to …," "My greatest strength is …" (Mazza, 1999, p. 165) and "If I weren't so (fill in emotion), I. …" Adams (1998, p. 16) provides some additional stems that might further tap beliefs about oneself:

A word that describes me is …
I am a person who …

If I had time I would ...
I am grateful for ...
The person I feel closest to is ...

Exercise 5: Identity and Meaning Exploration. These exercises delve more deeply into how the individual views the self by providing items that focus on self-definition, purpose, and desires. The client is asked to answer each of these items with only one or two short sentences:

Who am I?

Who am I?
What words would others use to describe me?
Words I would use to describe:
    My appearance ...
    My voice ...
    The way I think ...
    My emotions ...
    My family roles ...
    The type of friend I am ...
    The type of lover I am ...
    The type of person I am in the world. ...
What parts of myself do I reveal to others, and what parts do I keep to myself?
What parts of myself have I shed over time, and what parts have I kept?
Who am I becoming?

Why am I here?

Why have I been put on this planet at this exact moment in time?
What is my purpose?
How do I know?
Do I have something to learn or to teach?
What brought me here?
Have I been prepared somehow for being here right now?
What can I gain from being here now?
What can I offer to others while being here now?
Do I want to stay here?
If so, what are my goals?
If not, where do I want to go next?

What do I want?

What do I want during my time here?
What are my highest goals for myself?
What do I want most for others?
What are my greatest hopes for the world?

What do I want to accomplish?
What do I want for my future self?
Do I have what I want?
Do I want what I have?
How close am I to my ideal life?

>**Clinical example:** *DeAndre came to therapy because his girlfriend said if he didn't see someone to get help with his problems, their relationship could be over. At first, DeAndre didn't have much to say in session, other than that he wanted to save his relationship enough that he was willing to see a therapist. At the first session, it appeared DeAndre would terminate quickly. During the second session, DeAndre was asked to complete written answers in response to the three main questions, "Who Am I?" "Why Am I Here?" and "What Do I Want?"*
>
>*DeAndre complied and to his surprise, generated two pages of handwritten text within session. When discussing the main themes that arose with the therapist, he disclosed that he saw himself as the strong one in his family, and that he was put on this planet to protect and provide for his family members and keep them all together. As the eldest son, he believed he'd failed to protect his family when he witnessed his youngest brother die in an accident where he fell from a second-story window and should have "seen it coming because I was right there." Being the strong one, he also had to "hold it together" in front of his family and take over responsibility for his brother's funeral arrangements because his parents were so devastated. He also disclosed that as the strong one, he should show no weakness in front of his girlfriend because she would think less of him if he openly grieved in any way.*
>
>*By the end of the session, DeAndre was beginning to explore what he wanted in relation to his brother's death, his family members, and his relationship with his girlfriend, and how witnessing his brother's death had impacted him. Understandably, he initially focused on wishing his brother hadn't died and that he'd been able to stop it from happening. DeAndre nonetheless opened space within therapy to explore different goals, interaction patterns, and outcomes with important people in his life, while at the same time clearly stating how he sees himself.*

Exercise 6: Feelings Profiles. Adams (1998) suggests: "Make a list of feelings you know well ... make another list of all the feelings you only are acquainted with ... make a third list of feelings that you don't relate to or understand" (p. 57). Each feeling, whether or not it is related to trauma, can have its own list of associated physiological sensations, thoughts, and memories. Similar to suggestions found in Adams (1998), we present here a list of sentence stems that help the individual focus on one of the feeling states indicated in the generated lists above:

The three times when I've had this feeling the strongest are …
If I held this feeling in my hand, it would have the following:
    Weight …
    Size …
    Brightness. …
    Color and hue …
    Texture …
    Hotness/coldness …
    Shape …
The place my body holds this feeling the most is in my …
If this feeling could sing, it would sound like …
When this feeling talks, it says …
The way I usually deal with this feeling is …

> **Clinical example:** *Annabelle was a student majoring in chemistry who was somewhat constricted in affect. She had a difficult time identifying and naming her emotions and would often say she was "fine" or "upset" and had little vocabulary for exploring her emotions. After establishing rapport, the therapist began to address her reluctance to name her emotions (e.g., how she would say she was fine but look visibly depressed). Annabelle and her therapist agreed to try an exercise to help better identify and label her feelings. She needed a language for her internal states, and that is what this exercise aimed to do.*
>
> *Given her orientation as a scientist, Annabelle was able to relate to externalizing her feelings and imagining their more concrete properties, like color, weight, and size. By using her more concrete skills during this writing exercise, she was able to relate to her feelings on a more visceral level and recognize when certain feelings were coming up in session. This was crucial to the therapeutic process and also allowed Annabelle to feel a sense of mastery and safety in session.*

Exercise 7: My Body Speaks. Clients may benefit from becoming more aware of general body sensations through the use of specific sentence stem exercises. Mazza (1999) provides the sentence stem, "If my hands could speak. …" This can be adapted to other parts of the body to generate feelings and associations related to the body. For example, "If my eyes could speak …," "If my heart could speak …," "If my stomach could speak. …" It may be particularly salient to identify areas of the body that may hold a lot of tension, cause a sense of conflict/distress for the client, and/or are related to traumatic experiences.

Exercise 8: Beliefs (shoulds, musts, and oughts). This exercise is inspired by Mazza's (1999) suggestion of incorporating "shoulds, oughts, and musts" within family therapy, as well as work by Beck (1995), Janoff-Bulman (1989), and McCann and Pearlman (1990). Tapping into personal belief structures, clients can complete the following sentence stems: "I should. ... I must. ... I ought. ..." This same exercise may be repeated with "Others should. ... Others must. ... Others ought. ..." and "The world should. ... The world must. ... the world ought. ..." to clarify trauma-related beliefs regarding self, others, and the world.

Exercise 9: I wish. ... Completion of the sentence stem "I wish ..." and/or the series "I wish ..., I used to be ..., But now I ..." (Koch, 1970, as cited in Mazza, 1999, p. 37) can help clients build a future focus.

Exercise 10: If I could be. ... To encourage wishing and imagining future desired qualities/characteristics, clients can complete the sentence stems, "If I could be _____, I would ..." and "If I were _____, then I would. ..."

Relationships with Others

Exercise 11: Defining Relationships. This exercise allows clients to express beliefs around trust, initiating a relationship, and sharing intimacy. Responses can serve as a springboard for discussion about what may be useful in therapy and how the therapist can build rapport with a particular client. It also often reveals issues related to interactions with family, friends, and others in the client's life. The sentence stems are as follows:

I feel most comfortable with another when ...
Being open and honest can be ...
I feel most vulnerable when ...
For me to connect with someone means ...
Others can best have a deep conversation with me by ...
Others can best share closeness with me by ...
My trust is earned when ...
I would prefer you not ...
I would prefer you ...
I want ...
I can ...
I hope ...
We should ...
We could ...
Let's ...

Clinical example: Jameson was a 54-year-old veteran who wasn't sure how he felt about "this whole therapy thing." His entire body had a "hunkered down" appearance in session, and he was a man of few words. Writing wasn't something Jameson could envision himself doing. He tended to express himself by behavior—mostly staying home, withdrawn with a six-pack. The therapist decided to introduce writing with the use of sentence stems given their high level of structure and pacing. In order to work on engaging Jameson in treatment, he completed the above sentence stems.

By completing this exercise, the therapist was able to more fully understand what it took for Jameson to even come to a session. He was deeply averse to being close to someone, preferring to keep his "space." He didn't want to feel pressured to "express [himself]" and just wanted to have "a real conversation" with the therapist. For Jameson, respect was huge—he expected to be respected and also understood that respect is something someone has to earn. The therapist also learned that one of the goals Jameson wanted most was to have a sense of "peace" in his life and that he felt like he could be able to achieve things by setting his mind to it. This provided an excellent platform for discussions with the therapist around what a "real conversation" would look like and how Jameson would know whether he had attained a sense of peace in his life.

Exercise 12: A Focus on Others. An important part of trauma recovery is for individuals to reconnect with their communities and society after trauma (Herman, 1992). In order to help the client with this process, the following sentence stems orient the client toward family members and can be reworded to focus on friends, co-workers, and others within the community (Neimeyer, 1999). The following sentence stems help engage the client when using family as the topic

When I imagine family:

I see the color …
I hear …
The texture it feels like is …
It tastes like …
It smells like …
It makes me feel like …

Recall and Beginning Exposure

The sentence stem exercises that follow use "semi-guided free association" to aid in processing trauma. Memory is engaged to help clients integrate trauma within the overall story of their lives (Ford, Russo, & Mallon,

2007; Guterman & Rudes, 2005). The sentence stems presented here are designed to explore internal schemas related to intrapsychic, interpersonal-dyadic, relational, and family-sociocultural experiences (Magnavita, 2005). Clients may remember and mourn what was lost through traumatic experience (Herman, 1992) and reflect on changes and/or gains. Attention is also paid to the potential for life-enhancing spirituality and "posttraumatic growth" after trauma (Tedeschi, Park, & Calhoun, 1998, as cited in Neimeyer, 1999).

Sentence stem exercises in this section also address the past, present, and future. Clients reflect on the past by writing about their personal history and grief. Focus on the present is achieved through exercises that identify and explore current problem areas (Guastella & Dadds, 2006). Other exercises with a perspective toward the future may help engage clients in hoping and wishing, allowing them to further explore goals for their lives. According to May (1969), wishing and fantasy are needed components within the therapeutic context (as cited in Schneider, 2008), allowing individuals to think about life changes and possibilities.

Exercise 13: Problem Identification. Before creating a narrative with a beginning, middle, and end (past, present, and future: see later sections), we suggest that clients begin with sentence stem exercises that help identify problems, wishes, and desires. Mazza (1999, p. 165) provides the following sentence stems to explore unpleasant emotions in a spontaneous way. These may increase insight about trauma triggers and their contextual details:

I am most sad when …
I am afraid of …
I am angry about …
I am doubtful about …
I am hurt when …

Exercise 14: My Loss. This exercise is designed to help initial exposure to traumatic material that incorporates the past, present, and future in light of loss:

My loss is …
I used to feel …
Now I feel …
When I think of the future I …
Losing _____ was like …
Living without _____ is like …
My grief is …
An image symbolic of my pain is …
Three words that describe my pain are …

If I could say three words to the person or thing I have lost, they would be ...
To continue on, I must ...
I will try to ...

> **Clinical example:** *Armand lost his right arm in a motorcycle accident. His trauma work within therapy was greatly enhanced by incorporating a bereavement perspective. In trauma, loss is an essential issue, and many symptoms can be attributed to grief over not only what happened but feelings of loss from the experience. Armand's struggle with drinking and irritability began to improve after he was able to address the loss of his limb.*
>
> *With the use of writing, Armand was able to explore how the effects of trauma on his body were affecting him psychologically. Issues of personal agency and competency came to the surface as he wrote about the loss of his arm. He began to express the deep powerlessness and hopelessness that were fueling his drinking. This helped him to wonder about the role of drinking in his recovery, enhancing his readiness for change and identifying other ways of coping post-trauma.*

Exercise 15: Happiness, Goals, and Roadblocks. To hone in on goals, clients may complete the following sentence stems about when they feel most happy:

I feel most happy:
with myself when ...
at home when. ...
at work when ...
with my partner/significant other when. ...
with family when. ...
with friends when. ...
in the world when. ..."

Mazza (1999, p. 26) also suggests that clients complete sentence stems in order to help identify limited goals: "I would like to ...," "I keep on because ...," "Life would be better if. ..." We suggest the following sentence stems to help further identify future goals and possible roadblocks:

All would be better if ...
All would be resolved if ...
I'd prefer ...
My hope is ...
My dreams include ...
I wish ...

I need …
My goals include …
Things I can change include …
I need to …
If my problems were over, the things that would be different include …
When things are better, my family will …
When things are better, my friends will …
When things are better, I will …

Detailed Exposure

Clients are guided through their internal experiences while recounting traumatic memories using the sentence stems given below (Cahill et al., 2006). Clients are asked to describe physiological sensations, thoughts, and emotions during the process in response to specific sentence stems. Sensory, cognitive, and emotional recall is the goal (Onyut et al., 2005; Schauer et al., 2005). While doing imaginal exposure through completing this writing exercise, clients are also encouraged to identify and express thoughts that counter their original distress-maintaining beliefs (Shapiro & Maxfield, 2002).

Exercise 16: Trauma Details. The following sentence stems introduce clients to explicitly focusing on details of a traumatic event:

When I think of that trauma, I …
My earliest memory of that trauma is …
Thinking about it, my body feels …
Emotionally, I feel …
When I recall that trauma, the thoughts that come to mind include …
Other images that come to mind include …
Concluding this exercise, I think of a place where I feel safe and imagine …

Exercise 17: Identifying Exceptions. Clients identify and examine situations that constitute exceptions to the rule (Guterman & Rudes, 2005) in order to help increase mental and emotional flexibility. Relative to trauma, life experiences that embody exceptions are recalled (Note: "X" should be replaced with whatever clients are trying to find exceptions for):

As a result of trauma, it seems like X was always/usually the case, but when I think about it …
X did not happen when …
I felt differently when …

When this different experience happened I felt ...
When I didn't feel X, I. ...
Physically, I felt ...

My thoughts around this incident include ...

Factors that may have contributed to this different event or outcome include ...
Exceptions to the rule means that ...

Section 3: Acrostics and Poems

Acrostics

Moving from sentence stems to more free-form writing exercises, we suggest that acrostics and/or poems be the next type of writing task introduced by the therapist. For both acrostics and poem exercises, we recommend that no more than 10 to 15 minutes in session be spent on the writing task itself.

As clients become more engaged with and used to dealing with highly charged material in a written format, we maintain that poetry in multiple forms can be a nice bridge between the structure of sentence stem completion and the more open-ended narrative approaches presented in later sections. Acrostics constitute a structured form of poetry and seem to provide a frame that can be helpful for the beginning poetry writer. Acrostics are completed by writing the letters of a topic/word vertically down the page and starting each line with a letter in the topic/word (Adams, 1998). Here is an example using a variation of "home:"

> Hearing the station master,
> Open to the evening sky.
> Moving out, all of you ...
> Every soldier goes home today!

Here is another example using a variation of "rape:"

> Rescued by no one
> All alone
> Please never let this happen again
> Exiting life

As noted, acrostics can be used with any topic or word(s) relevant to clients. Below we provide a few suggested topics where the use of acrostics may be most helpful (moving from therapy itself to client internal states to others and the environment to a future focus). However, these are only suggestions, and the topic/word used for these exercises is limited only by the creativity of the therapist and client when collaboratively designing this type of writing task.

Exercise 1: Therapy. Clients write on the topic of "therapy" or another related word/phrase. Acrostics can be used for a wide variety of topics denoting therapy (e.g., "morning meetings"):

T …
H …
E …
R …
A …
P …
Y …

Exercise 2: "What's going on?" Clients complete an acrostic for what's currently going on using all the letters of the alphabet (Adams, 1998), or using the letters of a presenting issue or an identified problem:

C …
A …
N …
C …
E …
R …

Exercise 3: Current Feeling. An acrostic may be composed on a current emotional state, feeling (e.g., pain, guilt), or mood (e.g., sad, annoyed) by using all the letters of the alphabet written vertically down the page, or using the letters of the emotional state as shown below (Adams, 1998):

R …
E …
G …
R …
E …
T …

Exercise 4: My Body/Body Part. An acrostic is completed using the topic, "My Body" or any other particular body part that is most affected by client distress or is a focus of concern (e.g., stomach, head):

H …
E …
A …
R …
T …

68 Part III-I: Beginning Exercises

Exercise 5: Current Thoughts. The topic would be a word/phrase that reflects current thought processes related to self, others, the environment, or the trauma itself:

J ...
U ...
S ...
T ...
I ...
C ...
E ...

Exercise 6: What I Have Lost. The topic would be a word/phrase that denotes a lost part of the self or a lost loved one, thing, place, or dream for the future:

S ...
A ...
F ...
E ...
T ...
Y ...

Exercise 7: Family, Friends, and Others. For this exercise, others in the client's life are used as the general topic (Mazza, 1999), and clients may reflect on things or behaviors that describe others before, during, and after the trauma:

S ...
I ...
S ...
T ...
E ...
R ...

> **Clinical example:** *At the first mention of Gwen's mother, dysfunctional family dynamics came to the fore, with her mother playing the prominent role of a controlling and emotionally abusive parental figure. Gwen had mixed feelings regarding her mother and limited insight into the extent of how her mother was affecting her. Later in treatment, Gwen completed an acrostic using the term "mother," which provided some containment and structure while introducing her to poetic writing using spontaneous expression related to such a charged topic.*
>
> *After her first acrostic exercise, she proceeded to complete a more extensive one using the phrase, "m-o-t-h-e-r-k-n-o-w-s-b-e-s-t." Shortly*

after completing the second exercise, Gwen realized she didn't want to be as involved in her abusive family situation. She was tired of it and saw how it was putting a strain on her relationship with her boyfriend.

Her writing also uncovered how her mother's attitudes toward Gwen's social relationships affected her own views on peer relationships. Gwen was often very judgmental of herself and others, tending to withdraw socially when emotionally overwhelmed. She also saw how her trauma history was impacting her ability to be the kind of peaceful, social person she wanted to be. All of this was discussed over a few sessions with her therapist, using her writing as a tool to guide discussion.

Exercise 8: Hopes for the Future. The topic of this acrostic would include an identified goal or hope for the future (e.g., "healthy relationship"):

H ...
E ...
A ...
L ...
I ...
N ...
G ...

Poems

We now move from the structure of acrostics to the more free-flowing requirements of creating poems. Once again, we recommend that these poems be approached as a task where the first thing that comes to mind is written down and that no more than 10 to 15 minutes are taken within a session to complete the exercise. Below we suggest poetry topics that range from creating a safe place to personal feelings and thoughts to a more outward focus (people and environments to a focus on the future).

Exercise 9: A Stable Place. Similar to Mazza's (1999) suggestion to write about a relaxing place, Serlin (2008) highlights the importance of imagining a stable place. Write a poem detailing images of a stable place (e.g., a stable, safe room). Go into the minute details—for example include what one would find in the room (on a table/desk) and what your new roles would be in this place.

Exercise 10: Personal Island. Picture and write about your own personal island. Where is the island located? What does it look like? Is anyone on the island, or who would you leave the island to visit? This exercise may clarify issues of trust, safety, loneliness, and isolation for clients. Additionally, it may help construct an imagined safe place and identify clients' significant others.

Exercise 11: General Feeling Poems. When writing poetry about feelings, Adams (1998, p. 57) suggests two ideas: (a) "write a haiku (three-line poem of five, seven, five syllables) that crystallizes your feeling into one potent image," and (b) "think of an image or metaphor that represents your feeling and use it as the organizing theme of a poem."

Exercise 12: Working through Anger. Here we suggest a poetry exercise that focuses on anger. Below we provide two narratives that therapists can use to explain the topic, and to help clients write a poem about coping with angry feelings (one that focuses on self and one that focuses on someone else):

1 Many times you probably feel angry or frustrated about having experienced trauma in your life. Perhaps you feel deeply changed and are angry about the person you have become as a result. Many times people feel incapable of doing things they used to do, like feeling safe in the world or opening up in relationships. Your outlook about the future may have also changed. How has this affected you? Write a poem about these feelings, and take no more than 10 to 15 minutes to do so. Write whatever comes to mind.

2 Someone you know is angry about a trauma and is having difficulty coping. How would you help him or her cope with these feelings? Is there an activity or ritual you both could engage in to help release this anger? Write about this in a poem.

> **Clinical Example:** *Aleesha was extremely angry about the way she was treated by college officials after she reported being sexually assaulted during a college party on campus. She came to the campus counseling center to help deal with the disturbing emotions related to the sexual assault itself, as well as the abusive and dismissive way she'd been treated by the very people who should have had her best interests at heart. While much of therapy initially dealt with concrete strategies she could use in order to hold the perpetrator accountable, as well as the officials who failed her, she continued to report how her anger at the entire situation was negatively affecting her close friendships and more recently her school work. Aleesha was an individual who was a "doer" and wanted to know if there were things she could do to "get around it" so she could function better.*
>
> *Aleesha was asked to imagine what she would say to a close friend who was going through something similar, and she agreed to write a poem about how she would help her friend deal with the fallout. As a result, the writing exercise helped Aleesha to develop a different, more compassionate perspective on her own reactions and emotions, as well as to generate new coping strategies for herself.*

Exercise 13: Working through Grief. The following questions serve as prompts for poems to assist with mourning:

1 Place yourself in a position where you are the person who is grieving a loss. You might imagine this as a loss of someone in your life or perhaps the loss of your old self before the trauma. Maybe you are further along and are saying goodbye to that part of yourself that was traumatized. Attend to the feelings of loneliness or other feelings that arise in this state. What is different now that this person is gone? What do you miss? In a poem, express how his or her presence in your life affected you, and how the loss has impacted you.
2 Someone close to you has just lost a loved one. What could you do for, or say to, this person? Write a poem about these feelings, and take no more than 10 to 15 minutes to do so. Write whatever comes to mind.

Exercise 14: Symbolized Values/beliefs. Clients visualize symbols that represent an abstract quality or value (e.g., justice, goodwill; Gerard, 1961) and write a poem about these symbols. The poem might include how clients would act if they embodied that value (e.g., kind, compassionate, trusting, and so on), and how they would feel about themselves.

Self as a Symbol/belief. Clients characterize themselves and their qualities through metaphor or simile and compose a poem built on this symbol. The first line of the poem may start off by finishing a prompt, such as: "I am a/ an ..." or "I feel like a ... "

My body as a symbol. Clients can use metaphor to express feelings and thoughts related to their body image (e.g., description of body as if it were a house, what would it look like, where would it be located, etc.) (Mazza, 1999). A sentence stem prompting clients would be "My body is a ... (type of house, such as a fortress or ancient ruins)."

Hope as a symbol. Hope can be explored with the use of symbolic metaphor. What is hope? A medal? Laughter? A song? Think of some symbol for hope and write a poem developing this idea. An example from Emily Dickinson (Dickinson, 1993, p. 19) would be:

> *Hope is the thing with feathers*
> *That perches in the soul,*
> *And sings the tune without the words*
> *And never stops at all.*

Exercise 15: Understanding the Problem. Use of metaphor and simile can also help clients craft a portrait of the problem, thereby externalizing and increasing their understanding of struggles. Use of a simile in reference to the problem can be helpful by comparing two different things using "like" or "as." For example, one could write that "traumatic stress" is like a storm on the ocean, turbulent with no end in sight. This simile likens the experience of traumatic stress to being caught out at sea in the middle of a storm, evoking feelings of turbulence and being overwhelmed. The poem could build on a simile, incorporating even more similes and/or metaphors. The following questions can aid in this endeavor when creating poems:

1. Use your senses to create a picture of your problems. You can focus on one of these issues or just "traumatic stress" in general. What would the problem look like, smell like, taste like, sound like, and feel like? Write a poem using detailed descriptions of these senses.
2. If the problem were a person, what would it look like or talk like? How would it behave? What would its purpose be? Why would it be around? Write a poem describing this problem person.

Exercise 16: Coping with the Problem. The following questions may assist in creating poems about life after trauma, to broadly review personal reactions to what has happened and how one is coping without exclusively focusing on acceptance. Below is a suggested narrative for therapists that may assist with the poem writing process:

> Write a poem about how life has been after the trauma or traumatic period. What was it like at first? Were there feelings of numbing, shock, anger? Discuss how your life transformed and what every day has been like moving further away from that time. Has the way you relate to yourself and others changed? What are the ways you have found to live with what happened and the difficulties you've experienced as a result of trauma? Write a poem about how you've coped with these changes.

Exercise 17: Pros and Cons Related to the Problem. Here, clients will write a poem from the standpoint of thinking about the pros and cons of a situation. For example, when writing the "con" side in the aftermath of a car accident, one might write about fear of driving and leaving one's apartment. When writing about the pro side, this person might write about the depth of self-understanding gained from retreating from the world for a time. Both the pros and cons would be written about in the same poem. This can be accomplished by writing all the cons at once, followed by the pros, or by alternating the pros and cons within each major issue. Once again, the client should take no more than 10 to 15 minutes to complete the poem, writing down whatever first comes to mind.

Exercise 18: Compassion for Others. Questions aimed at increasing compassion for the problem can also serve as prompts for writing poems. The following questions encourage perspective-taking while completing this poem-writing exercise:

1. How do people react to those who have experienced trauma? Why might it be difficult for them to respond in helpful ways? Are they

uncomfortable with the trauma itself? Does it bring up memories of experiences they have had? Does the trauma stir up horror at the cruelty in life? How could they become more caring and supportive? Write a poem about why others may not be very compassionate with those who have experienced traumatic events.
2 Imagine you are talking with those who have had traumatic events in their lives and are experiencing symptoms of post-traumatic stress. Does it bring up feelings of sadness sometimes? Do you ever experience more positive feelings as a result of this discussion? How is it for you after you talk with someone about trauma? What might some of the challenging and rewarding aspects of this discussion be? Write a poem about talking to others about trauma.

Exercise 19: Disclosing to Others. The following questions aim to explore issues about disclosing trauma to others in poetic form and perhaps even increase communication about the client's problems:

1 Reflect on the secrets you've kept hidden inside. Perhaps your secret is that the trauma occurred or that you are struggling in certain ways because of what has happened. What has prevented you from sharing these things? Are you worried about what would happen to you or your relationship with the other person? Perhaps he or she would treat you differently, or maybe you are worried about having feelings of shame—that you are somehow marked by what has occurred. Write a poem about this.
2 Reverse your roles and imagine how you would react if someone told you about the same trauma and was having a difficult time. Would you try to comfort or counsel him or her in some way? Write a poem about what you would do.

Section 4: Five-Minute "Sprints"

Rationale for Writing "Sprints"

In this section, we move to more fast-paced and condensed versions of writing assignments in order to increase emotional and cognitive intensity for clients. With these exercises clients are asked to write responses to particular questions or on certain topics for the duration of five minutes, spontaneously writing as quickly as possible, without stopping (Adams, 1998). The expectation is that at least a page will be filled with single-spaced writing at the end of five minutes, with the goal of intensifying the cognitive and emotional material associated with traumatic events. Furthermore, by increasing the speed of the writing exercise to maximize spontaneity, it is hoped that self-censorship will be reduced. This may also help ready the client for the more in-depth and intense free-flowing writing exercises that follow.

Once again, therapists should monitor client reactions to earlier and slower-paced writing exercises (e.g., lists, sentence stems, acrostics, or poems) before increasing intensity by using the exercises in this section. Note, however, that many of the topics suggested here for five-minute sprints overlap with the topics found in earlier sections. Such overlap is deliberate and may help provide links within and across exercises, especially for topics that are particularly salient for each individual client.

Exercise 1: Grounding Questions. The following questions can help individuals write about neutral or positive topics in order to help them become used to the format of these fast-paced five-minute writing sprints. Although it seems to be beneficial in and of itself, this particular exercise can also be used to re-center, re-orient, or ground clients after an emotionally overwhelming writing experience (Adams, 1998). In such a case, therapists can suggest that clients write about something silly or irrelevant, and/or answer any of the questions below in the event that they seem emotionally overwhelmed by earlier writing activities:

- What was this past week like for me? What was the best/worst of the week?
- What is the weather like today? Does it remind me of anything?
- Did I have a good laugh today? When, where, and why?
- What seems to be taking all of my attention today? Why?
- What/who do I feel close to today?

> **Clinical example:** *Gerald was 16 years old and had been in therapy on and off for a few years following the discovery that his uncle was sexually abusing him. He didn't like therapy and made this quite clear to his therapist at the outset of treatment. One of the reasons he didn't like therapy was that in the past he had always left the session overwhelmed, sometimes leading to an episode of cutting. Therapeutically, it appeared that the use of grounding was crucial in Gerald's recovery. He needed to feel safe in treatment and have appropriate closure and transition from sessions.*
>
> *After using somatic grounding techniques, like stomping his feet or rubbing his hands together, Gerald began to use sprint-writing techniques geared toward grounding. He was able to write out his reflections on the past week, transitioning toward the more immediate present with questions about what the weather was currently like. By using such sprint-writing exercises, he began to trust more in the therapeutic process, as he wasn't leaving sessions in a state of physiological arousal, and his cutting episodes post-sessions decreased.*

Exercise 2: Review of the Day. Clients may also obtain practice in completing a five-minute writing sprint, or attain emotional distance from intense experiences earlier in a session, by writing about their day: "Review your day from the time you opened your eyes this morning" (Adams, 1998, pp. 19–20). This question also helps individuals engage in chronological story construction, which can be a useful skill in recovery from intense thoughts and emotions, as well as provide practice in writing a story with a beginning, middle, and end.

Exercise 3: Experience of Therapy. Clients write for five minutes about their experience of therapy and the sessions they've had so far, which may be less intimidating than explicitly writing about the relationship with the therapist or any traumatic events themselves. This exercise may also prompt discussion about the process of therapy or relationship issues with the therapist.

> Clinical example: *Shekina was a woman in her 30s who was successful in her work. She seemed invested in giving the impression that she was independent and did fairly well for herself. She was impeccably groomed, educated, and spoke in an eloquent manner. The therapist found Shekina very likeable and charming, and there was a natural ease with Shekina, and warm smiles and sometimes laughter could be had in session.*
>
> *At about session six, Shekina completed an open-ended sprint writing exercise on her thoughts and feelings regarding therapy thus far. Shekina's responses came somewhat as a surprise given the mismatch with her presentation in session. Her writing revealed a deep sense of loneliness and feeling that no one could understand what she was going through. She felt isolated and unsure of how her therapist could help her. She expressed a deeply critical attitude toward the process of therapy and was wondering how many sessions she would need to truly address her symptoms.*
>
> *This piece of writing was a gift for the therapeutic process and served as a catalyst for change. Although Shekina could have chosen to write about the high-functioning part of herself, the sprint writing exercise seemed to tap into a part of her she tended to keep under wraps. Shekina and her therapist had thus gained access to these issues through her writing—a part of herself that felt despair, isolation, and loneliness and was very much connected to what had been experienced during multiple traumatic incidences in the past. Treatment was able to progress from that point, as Shekina's sprint writing exercise had accessed a different part of her that she had been unwilling to reveal in her usual day-to-day interpersonal interactions.*

Exercise 4: Current Feelings. As a five-minute writing sprint exercise, clients write a response to Adams' (1998, p. 20) direction: "Name a feeling you're having right now and explore it." Clients may also close their eyes, describe how they feel, and identify any images that arise (Gerard, 1961).

Expansion of this exercise could include reflecting on how current feelings were experienced throughout the day and/or writing about any chosen feeling by answering the question, "How did I experience _____ today?" (Adams, 1998, p. 57).

Exercise 5: Current Problems and What's Going on. Clients may write about the following topics for five minutes each: (a) main problems they are facing, and (b) what's going on for them in their lives right now.

Exercise 6: What I Wish Would Have Happened. Clients imagine what they wish had happened surrounding a traumatic event(s) and write about this in a five-minute time window.

Exercise 7: Positive Choice around Trauma. Clients identify any positive changes in themselves or in life direction (Guastella & Dadds, 2006) as a result of the trauma. The process of benefit-finding may assist in evaluating post-traumatic growth (Tedeschi & Calhoun, 1996). Importantly, those who are able to find meaning and possible benefits of tragedies are able to cope better than people who find no benefit (King & Miner, 2000, as cited in Pennebaker, 2004). Clients write about a positive choice or changes they have made surrounding the trauma, using whatever first comes to mind, in a five-minute timeframe.

Exercise 8: Hopes and Finding Life Meaning. Clients explore and express their hopes and desires for life and the future in five minutes. Additionally, Bunting and Hayes (2008, p. 233) suggest that asking clients, "What do you want your life to stand for?" helps clarify the client's definition of a meaningful life.

> *Clinical example:* Katie was an upperclassman in college preparing to enter "the real world." She grew up in a chaotic household witnessing domestic violence. She knew she wasn't happy with how things had been going for her and struggled to stay in control of her alcohol and marijuana use, especially during parties and other sorority functions. Indeed, Katie had been to rehab toward the end of high school and had been ambivalent about higher education from the beginning. She struggled with feelings of self-confidence and personal agency, feeling instead at the mercy of her "impulsivity." Katie would often spend large amounts of money on booze, marijuana, and clothes shopping in order to maintain her high status within her sorority. She wasn't really sure where she was going and felt lost. After completing a sprint-writing exercise in response to the question, "What do I want my life to stand for?" she connected with a higher functioning part of her identity and anchored herself in her strengths.

Katie was able to see that she wasn't just a "slacker" or "too messed up" to succeed. She connected with her values and humanitarian interests, helping to elevate herself from a place of shame to an appropriate level of high standards for herself, noting her many accomplishments so far. Shortly after completing this exercise in session, she reported decreased impulsivity, practicing more mindfulness on a daily basis. She appeared to realize that her less adaptive behaviors did not define her and what choices she was going to make in her life.

Part III-II
Intermediate Exercises

This portion of the workbook presents intermediate-level exercises that require clients to begin using more free-flowing writing skills while still providing a level of structure. Writing letters, composing eulogies, and creating character sketches and dialogues help clients become used to expository writing.

Once it appears that beginning writing exercises (lists/clusters, sentence stems, and so on) have been a good fit with the client, moving to more expository tasks can be helpful in terms of increased exposure to trauma issues, as well as externalizing these issues for more examination. Some of the writing exercises found here may also be helpful when individuals don't know where to start, when they don't want to get overwhelmed, and when they want to focus on one area (Adams, 1998).

Section 1: Letters

Once again, this group of exercises is meant to start slowly, where clients are at first asked to write short cards and/or letters to self or others in a more superficial way, and then move to more in-depth exercises. The exercises shown here can be in a very short format (no more than a single-spaced half-page of text taking up to five minutes to write), to medium-length formats (a single-spaced full page of text that takes no more than 15 minutes), to longer formats (multiple page single-spaced letters that can be finished as between-session assignments). As always, the format for each exercise is limited only by the creativity of the client and therapist.

Exercise 1: Holiday Cards. Clients are asked to write a holiday card (including birthdays or important anniversaries) addressed to themselves, someone they have lost, or to someone who has hurt them (Mazza, 1999). They may also write, then discard a holiday card to someone who is unavailable regarding unfinished business relating to the trauma. If completed in session, these cards should consist of no more than a single-spaced half-page of written text, and take no more than five minutes to complete. To assist in completing the exercise, you may ask clients to imagine a "Hallmark Moment" that is humorous, touching, dark, sarcastic, and so on.

Exercise 2: Letters to Self. Clients are asked to write a letter to themselves using the prompt, "What do you want your past, present, or future self to know about X?" (Note: X would be whatever the salient issue is at the moment). The letter should be no more than a single-spaced page of text at first and take no longer than 15 minutes to complete. However, this exercise can be expanded in terms of page length and time taken if it appears to be helpful for the client. In addition, clients can complete all three separate letters that address the past, present, and future self, if this exercise especially resonates.

Exercise 3: Dear Problem. Externalization of the problem can be achieved by giving the problem a name and writing it a letter (Carr, 1998). This letter could be addressed to a place, an object, a timeframe, a person, or a group of people (whatever the client identifies as being problematic in the moment). Once again, this letter should be no more than a single-spaced page of text at first and take no longer than 15 minutes to complete. However, this exercise can be expanded in terms of page length and time taken if it appears to be helpful; multiple letters to a series of different problems can also be completed.

Exercise 4: Letters to Important Others. Writing assignments can be employed to help survivors validate their changed identities among their social connections (Neimeyer, 1999), and educate important others about their new beliefs and views. Clients may write many different types of letters to other people expressing unspoken emotions and goals, and how they've changed through the process of surviving the trauma.

However, while sharing the effects of trauma with others has been found to be beneficial in some treatment settings (Fallot & Harris, 2002; Ford & Russo, 2006; Ford, Russo, & Mallon, 2007), Gidron, Peri, Connolly, et al. (1996) found that some clients became more depressed after disclosure to others (as cited in Pennebaker, 2004). Pennebaker (2004) also warns against unintentionally humiliating the survivors when trauma writings are shared, and urges that writings remain private. Given mixed findings about sharing trauma with others, caution should be used when deciding to share writings. Careful planning should involve a cost-benefit analysis of sharing, and assessing safety and trust in the relationships with the intended audience. Thus, for the exercises in this section, we suggest that clients write letters to others with the assumption that they will not be given to the person they are addressing. If clients wish to give the letters to others, the therapist and client should discuss in depth the possible ramifications of doing so.

Letters to others may be addressed to a whole host of individuals who have impacted the clients' life, for good or ill. Here is a list of people clients may wish to address during this writing exercise: (a) helpful, supportive others, (b) others who have been unsupportive or discounting, (c) others who don't know about what happened and are hearing about it for the first time, and (d) others who caused the trauma. Such letters can begin using the prompt, "What do you want X to know about Y?" (Note: X would be the person being addressed, while Y would be whatever the salient issue is at the moment).

As noted, this letter should be no more than a single-spaced page of text at first and take no longer than 15 minutes to complete. However, this exercise can also be expanded (page length and time taken) if it appears to be helpful. Multiple letters to a series of different people can also be completed.

> **Clinical example:** *George was a doctoral student finishing the coursework for his degree. He presented in treatment for help coping with his mother's terminal illness. In the course of therapy, George grappled with whether to return home in the middle of his last semester of classes to assist his family in taking care of his mother, who was in the final stages of dying from cancer. George expressed feelings of guilt for being removed from his family during this time and didn't know how to proceed.*
>
> *He expressed frustration toward his family, too, for not seeming to acknowledge his mother's illness and sometimes pretending that she wasn't dying. He explained that no one discussed his mother's impending death, least of all with him when he called home or e-mailed family members about her illness.*
>
> *During therapy, letter writing was a way for George to connect with the language of his feelings and provide a forum to confront his family members with these feelings (these letters were not shared with his family). Later, he composed a letter to his mother about the things he wished to tell her; this included thoughts and feelings that he wished to share before she died, and also about how losing her was affecting him. When George decided to write this letter, and then read it out loud in session, it was transformative for him because his mother's illness had advanced to the point where she was often unconscious, preventing him from communicating with her before she died.*

Exercise 5: Advocacy Letters. Clients may write a letter to individuals who are in a position to make policy, political, monetary, or programmatic social changes that reduce the chances of negative outcomes in the future. Such individuals may include state or federal senators or congress people, the president of a university, the local chief of police, and so on. The point of this exercise is to use client experience to advocate for social change on behalf of themselves and others, as well as bring awareness to powerful others about issues they have faced as a result of trauma (e.g., safety of a particular area of town, gun control, campus sexual assault, and so on).

Exercise 6: Accepting Trauma. The following prompts are designed to generate internal tension for change and healing post-trauma:

> What would it mean for me (or others) to *accept* my past trauma? What are some reasons I (or others) wouldn't want to accept what happened? What would acceptance look like? How would my life look different—would I act differently and/or would others act differently toward me? What are my concerns about this? What are the feelings that come up as I imagine this? What are some reasons it might be better to accept the trauma versus the alternatives (e.g., ignoring it or getting "stuck" on it)? Write a letter to yourself or someone else based on these reflections.

Section 2: Obituaries and Eulogies

While these types of exercises generally constitute shorter writing tasks than composing letters, they appear to be more pointed and intensely focused on loss, whether the loss be of a another person, place, thing, or a past personal identity that has been changed as a result of trauma. This is why we have chosen to place these exercises after the letter writing section. Once clients have become comfortable with letter writing, they may be willing to turn to exercises that are more explicitly focused on loss.

These exercises generally take two forms: (a) short life summaries based on formats found in obituaries, and (b) longer eulogies (life summaries) based on formats found in speeches given at ceremonies that mark transitions/loss (e.g., funerals). For the obituary format, newspapers and other media outlets usually constrain submissions to about 500 words in length (or about one-half of a single-spaced page). For all of the suggested obituary-writing exercises below, this same format should be used.

On the other hand, eulogies are usually much longer and depend on the time given for the speech, the type of venue in which the eulogy will be given, and other constraints. We recommend that for the first attempt at creating a eulogy, writing should be constrained to one page of single-spaced text. The exercise can be expanded if the client finds the exercise helpful and the exposure to loss is not too distressing. Furthermore, the client and therapist can decide if it would be helpful for the speech to be delivered out loud, either alone or with someone else (such as the therapist) after each eulogy has been written.

Obituaries

Exercise 1: Obituaries for Self. Clients can be asked to recall obituaries they have seen in the past and note the items that are usually included. Some obituaries simply list birth and death dates, family members (predeceased and living), employment, interests, cause of death (sometimes), and information about memorial services, if any. However, there are many types of obituaries that expand well past this general outline, with some that are humorous, loving, biting, sarcastic, and so on. Clients are asked to compose an obituary that uniquely reflects their tone and style in relation to:

- Past self
- Present self
- Future self

Any or all of these may be written in any combination (Bunting & Hayes, 2008; Schneider, 2008). Bunting and Hayes (2008) also suggest that clients may write out what they would most like to see on their tombstone. Clients may then respond to the following questions (Schneider, 2008, pg. 93):

> What thoughts or feelings did it bring up regarding how you used to live/are currently living/want to live your life? What impact might it have on how you will continue to live now? What does your obituary say about time, aging, and death? What fears and priorities does it highlight?

Writing an obituary for the past self may help clients anchor their self-concept in a "before and after trauma" timeline, while writing an obituary for the future self may help create a vision of where they'd like to be post-trauma (e.g., definition of a "full life"). Writing an obituary for the present self can also assist clients in identifying where they are now or how they view themselves at the moment.

Exercise 2: Obituaries for Others. Similar to writing self-obituaries, clients are asked to create an obituary for another person. Clients are to compose an obituary that uniquely reflects their tone and style in relation to the following suggested list (non-exhaustive):

- A family member you love and cherish
- A good friend
- A co-worker or boss
- A beloved pet
- A person who hurt you
- Other people who have had an impact on you, for good or ill

Any or all of these may be written in any combination. Writing an obituary for another person, beloved or despised, may help clients externalize feelings and thoughts about important people and to gain perspective about possible losses. Such perspectives may bring to light feelings and thoughts of deep sorrow, regret, wishes for revenge, or even relief at the prospect of another's death. To help clients organize thoughts and feelings that arise with this exercise, they may be encouraged to respond to the following questions:

> What thoughts or feelings did it bring up regarding the loss? What impact might it have on how you will continue to live now? What does this obituary say about the other person's time, aging, and death? What fears and priorities does it highlight? If you felt anguish or relief (or some combination of both), what does that mean for you?

Eulogies

Exercise 3. Eulogy for Self. Similar to obituary writing exercises, clients can be asked to recall eulogies they have heard or read in the past and note the topics that are sometimes included. Eulogies can be humorous, loving, dark, sarcastic, and sometimes a combination of all of these. Clients are asked to compose eulogies that uniquely reflect their tone and style in relation to:

- Past self
- Present self
- Future self

As noted, we recommend that the first eulogy should be no longer than one page of single-spaced text, while the exercise can be expanded later if the client finds the exercise helpful. Writing a eulogy requires clients to identify their own major life themes (highly personalized), while memorializing their own challenges, personalities, accomplishments, and impact on the world.

Writing a eulogy for the past self may help clients identify major themes that are no longer salient in their current lives as a result of trauma and demark when and how their past self "passed away," while writing a eulogy for the future self may help create a life narrative of where they hope to be at the end of their lives. In contrast, writing a eulogy for the present self can also assist clients in identifying where they are now and what they might like to see change.

Exercise 4. Eulogy for People, Things, Places, and Events. Once again, clients are asked to recall eulogies from past experience and to create a eulogy for another person, thing, place, or event. Clients are asked to write a eulogy that reflects their own tone and style in relation to the following lists (non-exhaustive):

People
- A family member who you love and cherish
- A good friend
- A co-worker or boss

- A beloved pet
- A person who hurt you
- Other people who had an impact on you, for good or ill

Things
- A cherished possession that reminds you of good times
- A possession in your care (neutral or not)
- A memento of past trauma
- A piece of clothing you've had for years
- Any other thing that meant something to you, for good or ill

Places
- The house/neighborhood where you grew up
- Where you worked (first, current, last)
- Where you fell in love (first, current, last)
- Where you were when you first heard good/bad news
- Other significant places in your life

Events
- Major positive milestones (births, graduations, weddings, and so on)
- Major losses (death, trauma, injury, and so on)
- Other major events that had an impact on you, for good or ill

Any or all of these may be written in any combination. Similar to obituary writing, creating a eulogy for another person may help clients externalize feelings and thoughts about important people. Perspectives on loss relative to things, places, and events may also bring to light feelings and thoughts about the transient nature of life.

> **Clinical Example:** *Demetrius was struggling with rejection from his family after coming out to them as a gay man. While he had kept this part of himself secret from them for many years, he was in a serious relationship and contemplating marriage, and he wanted them to be more of a part of his life (and possible wedding plans). After he told his mother, she told his two sisters before he had a chance to talk to them. His mother and two sisters were deeply religious and very active in his hometown church; they told everyone there that Demetrius was no longer part of the family. Privately, they told him he was going to hell, he was no longer welcome at family functions, and should stay away from his nieces and nephews.*
>
> *During therapy, Demetrius disclosed he was part of an extended "chosen" family of fellow gay men and lesbians. His chosen family members were deeply supportive and had been with him through thick and thin. When asked what his chosen family thought of his birth family's reactions, he said they were equally aghast and commiserative,*

using biting humor and sarcasm to lift his spirits. Demetrius agreed to have members of his chosen family help him write a eulogy to his "old self" (pre-coming out) as if his mother and sisters were writing it. The result was a hilarious and scathing indictment of his old hidden self (as well as his mother and sisters) that Demetrius reported he'd read out loud at a friend's recent birthday party, where everyone knew what had happened. This helped him ritualize the loss of his old identity, as well as the loss of his birth family, with the help of his support structure.

Section 3: Character Sketches

We now suggest moving from short obituaries and longer eulogies to more descriptive and expository writing exercises using character sketches. This can be especially helpful for clients who experience alienation from different parts of the self. Indeed, van der Hart, Nijenhuis, and Steele (2006) discuss how being traumatized is often accompanied by dissociation and possibly a division of the personality. The authors identified disintegrated parts of the personality as the emotional part (EP) and the apparently normal part (ANP) (van der Hart et al., 2006). This may explain why the concept of parts and the use of parts language can be important in trauma treatment.

Character sketch exercises can focus on parts of the personality, or personify different aspects of experience that may be split off from integrated consciousness. Clients may explore themselves, certain feelings, people, topics, or objects by writing about their qualities or attributes (i.e., character). The writing instructions given below can help guide clients to write a character sketch:

> Now close your eyes and imagine this entity or person (self or something/someone else). What is the first thing you notice? Describe physical attributes or manner. How does the person speak, walk, act? What are his or her needs, dislikes, or fears? Feelings? What are your issues of conflict with this entity? What is its purpose or role in your life? What message does this have to give to you or others?

In general, character sketches constitute a longer writing task than seen in earlier sections of this workbook. Each sketch should be between one and two pages of single-spaced text and can take up to 20 minutes or longer to complete. These sketches can also be assigned for clients to complete between sessions. As before, the exercises in this section start with focus on the self, then move outward to focus on others, the environment, and events.

Exercise 1: Exploration of Parts of the Self. Clients are asked to provide a character sketch (using the instructions above) about various parts of their personality that may be higher functioning or conversely that may impede progress (e.g., "Old Self," "Scared Child," "Destroyer," "Controller," "Intimacy-Seeker," "Workaholic," and so on). One of the aims of this exercise is to increase awareness of the factors that maintain maladaptive behaviors, as well as to identify strengths. It may also be helpful to complete multiple sketches, one for each of the most salient parts of self. Further exploring how these parts fit together and/or interact may be helpful for the client. This can also presage the exercises found in the later dialogue section, wherein different parts of the self may engage in conversation.

Exercise 2: A Feeling as a Character. Clients are asked to write about a strong feeling they have (positive or negative) as if it were personified in another person, animal, or inanimate object (Adams, 1998). This helps to externalize feelings, describe them in detail, and perhaps provide understanding about how they arose, any function they may have, and how to best deal with feelings that are overwhelming.

> **Clinical example:** *Maya was triggered by feelings of loneliness. This was particularly true when she did not feel supported and loved by her partner. Most of the time, Maya would understand her partner's perspective, but disagreements about certain personal and ideological issues hit a nerve. Feeling misunderstood would provoke a feeling of isolation and loneliness reminiscent of growing up in her invalidating home with narcissistic parents. Maya would enter a place of despair brought on by loneliness, where her partner would physically and emotionally seem miles away.*
>
> *In therapy, Maya's therapist suggested she complete a character sketch of her recurrent feelings of loneliness in her relationship. What surfaced shocked Maya. The entity that came to Maya in her reflections was not a fully human presence, but a female mythical presence resembling a sorceress. This person had a hardened gaze and was full of hate, retreating to life alone in the woods. The entity was fully self-sufficient but brutally enraged. She had no interest in human connection, preferring complete control over her affairs with no compromise. In fact, her desire for control bordered on destruction of those who caused her pain if it would give her a sense of having more control, granting a better existence in the face of despair.*
>
> *Through completion of the character sketch, Maya understood the feeling of loneliness really was a surface level of emotion covering deeper feelings of rejection, rage, and despair. Maya realized that these unexplored feelings were creating much conflict in her relationships, perpetuating grudges and prolonged fights as she felt a keen sense of disconnection and rejection whenever invalidation occurred. Maya understood that this character had preserved for her a sense of identity cohesion and control over the years, when she felt her needs disregarded by loved ones. This character also served to protect her against despair and annihilation by inhabiting a space of brutality and force. Indeed, Maya became more aware of how others could resort to violence out of a sense of betrayal and alienation.*

Slowly, she was able to work on strategies to reconnect with her partner when this character was triggered and took center stage. This allowed Maya to become more comfortable with her inner rage and despair, secondary to family of origin wounds. The externalization of this entity helped Maya to challenge her tendencies toward black-and-white idealization/devaluation of her partner when triggered. She was ultimately able to avoid falling into a prolonged state of dissociative emotional cut-off and rage, increasing constructive and healing instances of rupture and reparation with her partner. In fact, the improvements in this arena extended to her other relationships, allowing Maya to feel more interpersonally connected overall, particularly in the face of feelings of rejection or abandonment.

Exercise 3: The Ideal Person. Clients imagine the ideal person, someone they admire, or someone who embodies desired characteristics, and write a character sketch about them. This helps to identify how the clients may ideally want to be, what they want to do or say, and may assist in setting future goals.

Exercise 4: How Others See Me. Clients write a character sketch about themselves from someone else's point of view (Adams, 1998), clarifying potential insecurities and how they think others perceive their strengths and weaknesses. This can assist clients in identifying parts of themselves they'd like to change or improve upon, or parts of themselves they're proud of and would like to strengthen.

Exercise 5: People Who Make Me Mad. Clients write a character sketch of the people with whom they are angry (Adams, 1998). This exercise can serve many functions, two of which are highlighted here. First, this exercise may help clients pinpoint characteristics of people who are not helpful (perhaps even harmful) to be around in order to avoid similar people in the future (e.g., "an early warning system"). Second, it might be helpful for clients to explore if they have similar characteristics to those who make them mad; sometimes, the very things we see as negative in others are the same things we embody. This can aid in perspective taking and building self-awareness.

Exercise 6: Family and Intimate Others. Clients elucidate patterns of relatedness and explore others' perspectives by writing selected sketches of family members, parents, intimate partners, and friends.

Exercise 7: Places, Things, and Events. Clients can create sketches of inanimate objects or situations (places, things, traumatic events) using human descriptors, as if these objects were alive and had agency, personality, and specific qualities.

Section 4: Dialogues

Once clients are able to compose character sketches of self, other people, and objects/events, it is often helpful to ask them to then create dialogues amongst the characters. Adams (1998) recommends allowing at least 20 minutes for writing these dialogues, starting with a reflection on the client's relationship with the dialogue partner, and any questions or statements the client wants to address. She advises respecting silences and pauses, as well as asking "Is there anything else?" (Adams, 1998, p. 39) upon arriving at a natural stopping point. The dialogue should look like a script on the written page (see below for examples).

Exercise 1: Dialogue with Parts of the Self. Clients may write a dialogue between parts of the self that have distinct characteristics. Using a part of the self that has been identified as "The Nice One," we provide a dialogue example:

THE NICE ONE: You really don't want to hurt her feelings. That's mean.
ME: You know I can't do everything she asks. I should say no.

Exercise 2: Dialogue with an Emotion. Clients write a dialogue between themselves and specific emotions, particularly those clients find difficult to experience (Adams, 1998). Using the feeling of "happiness" as a character with which the client engages in a discussion, we provide the following example:

HAPPINESS: It's so nice to be around.
ME: Who knows when you'll be leaving this time.

Exercise 3: Speaking with My Body. Clients write a dialogue with their bodies, or particular body parts, or aspects that are causing distress (e.g., stomach, heart, face, illness, injury, surgery, sexuality, or body subpersonalities such as those that are related to addiction or weight). Adams (1998) states this exercise can help access innate wisdom or messages the body is trying to relay.

> **Clinical example:** *Gabrielle had become pregnant after much difficulty at age 41. She entered therapy roughly a year postpartum after experiencing marital strife and presented with postpartum anxiety and issues related to sexuality. Gabrielle was a survivor of childhood sexual abuse. She felt disconnected from her body and struggled with sexual arousal. This exacerbated decreases in sexual activity during the postpartum period and began to impact the relationship with her husband.*
> *In treatment, Gabrielle completed a written dialogue with her womb. Her writing reflected a sense of re-traumatization that had*

occurred through conception, delivery, and the postpartum period. Gabrielle had had several trials of in-vitro fertilization before conceiving. The procedures had affected her body and mind in ways she hadn't realized until she dialogued with this part of her body. The dialogue revealed feelings of invasion, intrusion, and anger largely from the medicalized procedures surrounding conception and delivery.

Gabrielle had also experienced her body's transformation during pregnancy as painful as she had body image concerns, and a high need to maintain a certain weight. During pregnancy, Gabrielle was no longer able to maintain the close control she held over her weight and body shape. She often felt powerless under waves of nausea and fatigue, along with the steady weight gain of pregnancy. Feelings of being out of control related to her body were heavily reminiscent of her experiences of past sexual, physical, and emotional abuse, draining her coping reserves.

By the time she delivered her child, Gabrielle had experienced months of anxiety, spanning from pre-conception through pregnancy, with a sense that her body had been "hijacked." Gabrielle's subjective sense of an invaded body was ultimately heightened during a protracted labor, compounded by a flight or freeze response in face of painful uterine contractions. Labor did not progress normally and stalled, prompting administration of Pitocin and an epidural. The epidural and anesthetic numbing of her lower half mirrored the physical and psychic numbing associated with her prior abuse. The baby became stuck in the birth canal but was successfully delivered with the use of forceps and vacuum. Conception, pregnancy, and birth had now been paired with feelings of fear and being out of control.

Her body no longer felt like her own, so it was no surprise that she was having difficulty with sexual arousal. Through written dialogue with her womb, she came to realize a sense of trauma had reoccurred there—invasive pre-conception procedures followed nine months later by a hasty, fear-filled, and intrusive medical evacuation of her baby. The sexuality Gabrielle experienced postpartum was not the integrated, mature sexuality she had cultivated over years with her husband. It had been replaced with a fragmented, split-off, and immature sexuality, perhaps harkening to the age she was at the time of the original abuse. The dialogue exercise began a process of healing and reconnection with this part of her body. Gabrielle began to honor her experience of medical trauma and understand how this and the hormonal experience of new motherhood were impacting her sexual sensations and drive.

Exercise 4: Speaking with One's Spiritual Self. Clients are asked to dialogue with the imagined spiritual self (Adams, 1998; Gerard, 1961). Similarly, Comas-Diaz (2008) suggests visualizing a meeting with your "inner guide."

Kelly (1941) explains that this inner guide is a wise, compassionate advisor who can be a person, animal, object, ancestor, or a religious or historical figure (as cited in Comas-Diaz, 2008). Here are a few sentence stems to prompt this exploration:

My guide is …
My guide's name is …
My guide's purpose is …

Adams (1998) suggests picturing one's guide before beginning to write. Comas-Diaz (2008, p. 106), based on earlier suggestions from Metzger (1992) and Rossman (2000), offered the following questions to facilitate inner guide meditation: "Where is your guide? Go there and let me know what you see. Is he/she/it communicating with you? How are you feeling? What do you want to do?" Based on this encounter, clients can write a dialogue with the inner guide using the voice of this inner guide to talk about a particular problem (Adams, 1998; Rossman, 2000, as cited in Comas-Diaz, 2008). The inner guide can also be referred to as "Inner Wisdom," a higher power, or one's "Internal Self-Helper" (Adams, 1998, p. 38).

Exercise 5: Conversation with a Trauma Memory. Clients write a dialogue with the memory of their trauma—this can provide some degree of emotional distance and clarify feelings related to the memory (Adams, 1998). The specific character in the dialogue could be the person or thing that hurt the client, or it could represent a place, situation, or event that is related to the trauma.

Exercise 6: Talking with a Lost Loved one. Clients are asked to dialogue with a lost loved one. This might help clients say what was left unsaid, give or receive an imagined apology, or come to terms with the fact that the person is gone. To be most effective, the client is asked to be as true as possible to the loved ones' actual words and belief structures during the written dialogue.

Part III-III
Advanced Exercises

Section 1: Narratives

For the advanced writing exercises in this section, we have moved from highly structured exercises through semi-structured writing, and have arrived at exercises that require clients to create stories with a timeline—that is, writing a story about a person, situation, or event that has a beginning, middle, and end. It should be noted that creating narratives as an exercise can take many forms, in that they can be broken down into sections (i.e., writing the end first, and then choosing whether to write the beginning or middle next, and so on), can be given a time limit or page limit (or not), and can be reviewed at later times in order to revise the story based on events or changes that have occurred since the client last engaged with the material. Thus, narrative writing exercises can be creatively designed by therapists and clients together in an almost unlimited way.

Once again, we recommend that for narrative exercises, clients begin with shorter, more time-limited tasks in order to become familiar with the narrative format. At first, writing a story with a beginning, middle, and end should take no longer than 20 minutes and fill no more than two single-spaced pages. Later, the exercise can be expanded in terms of time taken to complete, as well as page length, and can also be assigned as an exercise between sessions.

Topics chosen can also be virtually unlimited. However, we suggest that less intense topics be chosen at first in order to familiarize clients with the task (as seen below). At later times, topics can be assigned that focus on loss, traumatic events, and other emotionally laden issues. As more intense topics are addressed, therapists and clients may wish to design shorter story formats (time and page length) and build up to longer story arcs over time.

In addition, it seems important that clients understand the main point of these exercises—telling a story. Often, errors in spelling, sentence structure, and punctuation or other writing issues may create a situation where clients do not believe they can write well enough to complete the task. We suggest that clients understand that writing errors are part of the creative process, and if possible such errors should be ignored. Clients can be instructed to write their story as if they were telling it to a trusted friend or confidante, and to write as freely as possible without editing or worry about the quality of the writing.

If clients find difficulty in composing stories or deciding where to begin, together the therapist and client can discuss how to create an outline with three headings that are related to the chosen topic; each heading would reflect the main point relevant to the beginning, the middle, and the end of the story. For example, in writing a story about "my best friend," possible headings could include "when we first met," "how we were there for each other," and "the last time we talked."

Focus on Self

Exercise 1: Childhood. For this exercise, clients choose a topic from a pleasant situation or event from childhood (e.g., "my first ice cream cone," "my most liked toy," and so on). Clients can choose to write this from the perspective of self (first person), as another person involved in the situation (second person), or as an outside observer of events (third person).

Exercise 2: Being a Teen. Clients recall an event (positive or negative) from adolescence and write a story from beginning to end from the first, second, or third person perspective.

Exercise 3: An Adult Milestone. Here, clients choose a salient milestone in their adult lives and tell how it first began, what happened as the event unfolded, and what the ending was like. If the impact of the milestone is ongoing, clients will choose an endpoint that is to their liking. Once again, they can tell the story from the first, second, or third person voice.

Focus on Others

Exercise 4: Family. For this exercise, clients choose an important person from their family who was a parent, sibling, grandparent, aunt/uncle, guardian, or other caregiver. Once the person is identified, clients remember an important event where that person was the main character in the story. Again, the narrative can be from the first, second, or third person perspective.

Exercise 5: Intimate Others. Clients choose a person with whom they've been romantically intimate (spouse, significant other, boyfriend/girlfriend) and recall an important situation or event where that person was the main character in the story, told from either the first, second, or third person perspective.

Exercise 6: Friends and Important Others. In this type of narrative exercise, clients will choose a close friend or other person who has had an impact on them. Once again, clients will remember an important situation or event where that person was the main character in the story.

Focus on Trauma

Exercise 7: Traumatic event. A narrative can be written about a specific traumatic event. The event could be the first of its kind, the worst, or perhaps the most recent. In any case, the client will choose the traumatic event that most stands out for them and choose a point in time that marks the beginning, the middle, and the end of the event. We recommend that when clients first engage in creating this type of story it be told from the perspective of a third person observer and be shortened in both time taken to complete and page length. This constrains the amount of exposure to potentially intense and upsetting material and allows both client and therapist to gauge the effects. Later assignments can be lengthened based on client reaction.

The importance of creating a story of one's trauma is supported by research suggesting that narrative construction is essential to trauma processing (Amir et al., 1998; Foa et al., 1995, as cited in Amir et al., 1998; Ford & Russo, 2006; Guterman & Rudes, 2005; Lamb, 2003; Pennebaker & Seagal, 1999). In the tradition of these findings, the following exercise includes instructions on how to construct a written narrative of past trauma. This narrative will include a description of the setting, main characters, event, immediate and long-term consequences, and overall meaning of the story. It may be simplest to write about single event traumas given the short writing time frame. For complex trauma, therapists and clients may tease out isolated traumatic incidents to serve as the focus for each written story. Therapists may want to be particularly alert for cognitive errors (e.g., "mind reading") when discussing client thoughts about the perspectives of other people. The goal is to remain flexible about different *possible* perspectives of others:

> Find a comfortable location for about 20–25 minutes to write the story of your traumatic experience(s) and any related thoughts. You may prefer to type on the computer or to write down the story with paper and pencil. Take a deep breath and write continuously without stopping for the full 20–25 minutes. Realize that you can take a pause from writing if you become too distressed and return to writing later.
>
> Try to turn-off your inner critic and let the writing flow spontaneously. Attempt to really connect with your most intimate thoughts and feelings. Remember this writing is for your eyes only.
>
> Focus on creating a story with a beginning, middle, and end. Be flexible about how the writing unfolds and don't judge yourself on style or grammar. Be specific in details that you recall and explain how you felt while the trauma occurred. Attend to and express the feelings that

are brought up now when recalling what happened. Are there ways in which you are responsible for some of the effects of the trauma?[1] What are some of the losses or gains that resulted from what happened? Can you think of any subsequent consequences or benefits? What have you learned?

Discuss the impact of this trauma on you and others. Relate the trauma to past relationships and events. How did it affect your relationship to yourself, others, and the world? What might others involved have been thinking and how would they convey their viewpoint on what happened? How might your behaviors have impacted others?

Begin to shift your focus to the present and how these past events have most affected you currently. How does it affect how you will relate in the future? How has the trauma affected the way you act and think about the past, present, and future? What meaning does this event have? Explore different viewpoints and perspectives. Try to finish writing anything that you haven't yet dealt with in your narrative or anything that would help you bring the story to an end.

Clinical example: *Bryan was 32 years old when he entered therapy, after having a series of long-term relationships with older women. He described these relationships as tumultuous, with Bryan always feeling like the pursuer. When discussing his relationship history, it became evident that Bryan had a traumatic first love relationship. The two met in high school, both coming from abusive backgrounds. They often bonded over this shared history, and ended up playing out many of their dysfunctional family of origin dynamics with each other.*

At 18, he and his girlfriend had a difficult time managing the anxiety arising from these struggles. They would go days without talking and then passionately reunite. Bryan saw his girlfriend for the last time during a spring break in college. He had gone to visit her at her school only to come face to face with more fighting, rejection, and the discovery that she was heavily abusing cocaine. It was devastating to Bryan that she had been leading a secret life for some time, and was in serious jeopardy of failing out of college.

Bryan's visit culminated in trauma. After a morning argument, he ran out of the dormitory to accompany his girlfriend to class and turning the corner in the street saw that she had been fatally hit by a car. He never had closure from this event, and the questions replayed in his mind about what he could have done differently in the relationship, or maybe what he could have done that morning to help her leave the

---

1 For this question, ideally the person would be able to understand the role of will and personal choice in how they respond to people and events in their lives. Otherwise this question may trigger maladaptive thinking (e.g., self-blame and depressive cognitions.)

dorm less upset. In his mind, he feared the argument made her so upset that she hastily crossed the street without looking. He would never know the answers to these questions.

By writing the narrative of this traumatic event, Bryan was able to organize his memories and form meaning around what had happened. He explored feelings from the time of this traumatic event that he had completely shut off for years. Bryan began to realize that the traumatic loss of this first love and unresolved grief had been haunting him throughout future relationships. He engaged with people who, much like his first girlfriend, could not truly emotionally support him and were often absent. Bryan began to take responsibility for the impossible expectations he had of women, perpetuating unhealthy dynamics and leading to devastating breakups. He realized he was repeating a sense of traumatic loss with each of these women to gain a sense of mastery and meaning over what had originally happened. Through his narrative writing, Bryan constructed meaning around this first romantic relationship and how it affected him. This relationship and loss became connected to the overall fabric and story of his romantic relationship history. He was able to relate what happened to his present struggles and what it meant for him moving forward in future relationships. Instead of being a split off horrifying event from his past, Bryan was able to create a new sense of meaning around this relationship, as well as a narrative with its own ending.

Exercise 8: Reactions of Others. For this exercise, the client chooses to write a story about a witness to the traumatic event, or a person who was told afterwards about the event and denotes this person's reactions. For example, a story could be created about a friend or family member who was told about the trauma, and their reactions are then written about in story format (beginning upon first disclosure with a middle and an end).

Exercise 9: The Aftermath. ... The clients choose to write about how their lives in general have changed as a result of the trauma. The topic could be anything related to loss, grief, growth, or changes for the better. Once again, a first, second, or third person perspective can be chosen.

Exercise 10: The Future. For this exercise, clients will choose a topic that will have an ending projected into the future, reflecting hopes and dreams. For example, the beginning of the story can be the trauma event itself, the middle of the story could be where the client is now in relation to the chosen topic, and the ending can represent the hoped-for outcomes as a result. (Note: this technique of projecting the ending of the story into the future can also be used with narrative exercises presented earlier in this section.)

Section 2: Essays and Compositions

This section of advanced writing exercises is even less structured than that found with narrative writing. Whereas narratives require a story told with a beginning, middle, and end, the exercises presented here simply require focused writing that targets a particular topic, with no imposed structure. The only requirement is that clients address a particular topic *relative to trauma* for each exercise. Similar to creating narratives, essays and compositions can take many forms, can be given a time limit or page limit (or not), and can be reviewed at later times in order to revise the material based on events or changes that have occurred. As with narrative exercises, essays and compositions can be creatively designed by therapists and clients in an unlimited way.

Again, we recommend that for these exercises, clients begin with shorter, more time-limited tasks in order to become familiar with essay and composition writing. At first, these tasks should take no longer than 20 minutes and fill no more than two single-spaced pages. Later, the exercise can be expanded in terms of time taken to complete and page length.

Topics chosen can be virtually unlimited. However, we suggest that less intense topics be chosen at first in order to familiarize clients with the task (as seen below). Similar to creating narratives, clients should understand that the main point of essay and composition exercises is to write about the issues that are most salient to them. Clients should understand that writing errors are part of the creative process, and such errors should be overlooked.

Focus on Self

Exercise 1: Essays about Positive Emotions. Those who use more positive emotion-words and causal, insight words have obtained greater benefits from writing (Pennebaker, Mayne, & Francis, 1997, as cited in Pennebaker, 2004; Pennebaker & Seagal, 1999). In their study, Pennebaker and Seagal (1999) found those who benefited most from writing tended to use many positive emotion words (e.g., happy, laugh), a moderate amount of negative emotion words (e.g., sad, angry), and an increase in the use of insight (e.g., understand, realize) and causal words (e.g., because, reason). Pennebaker (2004) also observed that the ability to acknowledge positive emotions when coping with trauma is related to optimism and benefit-finding. Additionally, he states that the use of "story-markers" or causal and insight words points to the ability to externalize the trauma, as well as gain perspective.

Often, when remembering traumatic experiences and the aftermath, clients have difficulty identifying any positive emotions, behaviors, qualities, or outcomes related to the event. The following list is provided to aid clients in identifying any positives when completing this exercise:

> Brave, safe, appreciative, affection, stable, relaxed, protected, confident, funny, agreeable, pleasant, lovely, wonderful, reconciled, harmony, grateful, comfortable, at ease, mild, tender, kind, faith, hope, attractive,

appealing, sweet, loving, pleased, honored, delighted, fulfilled, respectable, virtuous, worthy, blameless, adoration, tenderness, fondness, inspirational, motivating, exciting, pleased, fulfilled, pleasurable, blissful, amusement, enjoyment, resilient, powerful, tranquil, composed, soothing, unspoiled, impeccable, lively, cheerful, prepared, kind, respect.

We also suggest using the following therapist script when introducing this essay/composition task to clients:

> Here is a list of positive words (using the list above or a similar list of the therapist's own devising). You can use this list to identify something positive that has arisen from trauma experiences. At first, you may find it difficult to identify anything positive at all. You can begin to challenge negative words by lessening their intensity (e.g., "uneasy" instead of "afraid" or "glum" instead of "depressed") and then adding more positive words to your essay. Write the first thing that comes to mind and then expand on any positives you find.

Clinical example: *Tanya was in her early 20s and had experienced years of physical and emotional bullying by peers growing up. She suffered from obesity from grade school through adolescence. Last summer she underwent bariatric surgery and lost a great deal of weight. Unfortunately, Tanya presented to treatment struggling with depression and interpersonal difficulties. Despite her weight loss, she still felt terribly unhappy and alone. She was plagued by heightened interpersonal sensitivity bordering on paranoia, always assuming that others were judging her. In fact, Tanya's narrative was one of victimization, and she saw everything through a negative lens, which was reflected in how she spoke about her life. To help reconstruct her personal narrative, Tanya completed the exercise above by challenging herself to use more positive words when writing about her past experiences.*

She began to write about positive aspects regarding her experience growing up, noting the bravery she exhibited in the face of bullying by peers. She also recognized that although school was often like a battlefield, she felt fairly protected and safe at home with her mother. She acknowledged gratitude for this relationship with her mother and how it allowed her to maintain hope during the years of being bullied.

Tanya also wrote about personal positive attributes she had growing up, despite feeling insecure about her weight. She realized that being bullied helped her to become more tender-hearted and compassionate toward others, leading her to pursue training to become a teacher. Through writing, she articulated that she was not to blame for how others treated her and that she was kind and respectful toward others despite enormous challenges.

At the same time that she focused on using more positive words in her narrative, Tanya challenged herself to decrease the intensity of negative descriptors. For example, instead of writing that she was "tortured," she chose to write "mistreated"; instead of articulating that others "caused her to become suicidal," she wrote that the aggression from others led her to feel less hopeful about her future. This exercise was pivotal in helping Tanya to shift a negative life narrative that was still impacting her and to open up to a less polarized perspective about her history, her identity, and her future.

Exercise 2: Exceptions to the Rule. Clients may write an essay about exceptions to the negatives in their life, allowing for longer reflection about the often ambiguous outcomes of traumatic experiences. We suggest using the following therapist script to help clients begin this essay/composition exercise:

Identify a time when the negative aspects of trauma were not occurring in your life. Describe this experience by using one of the questions below. If you can think of other experiences that deviate from the way the effects of trauma are usually experienced, go ahead and write about these as well. Looking back at these exceptions to the rule, what factors were present that may have contributed to these different experiences or outcomes? Write an essay addressing these questions.

- When have you not felt _____? or When did _____ not happen?
- What was that experience like for you? How did you feel before, during, and after this experience?
- How did you feel physically before, during, and after this experience?
- What were your thoughts before, during, and after this experience?
- Was there any other time something similar happened and you didn't feel as you normally do or things didn't turn out how they usually seem to turn out?

Clinical example: *Farrah presented with sex addiction and a history of sexual trauma. As a child, she was sexually abused by an uncle who lived next door until she was a sophomore in high school. Beginning in middle school at the age of 12, Farrah exhibited sexualized behavior with her classmates and became precociously sexually active. By freshman year in high school, she was ridiculed by students in her school for being "loose" with guys, and she became involved in the drug scene. Throughout her later adolescence and into her twenties, she frequently found herself in risky situations with men. Abusive relationships began that initially started with emotional abuse, name-calling,* and controlling behavior, and frequently escalated to physical abuse and rape. By age 26, Farrah exhibited dependence on alcohol, and had a long history of abusive experiences with men.

The exercise above was used to help Farrah identify exceptions in her experience and to capitalize on potential factors leading to change. Through her writing, Farrah realized that many of her positive relationships with men happened at her job. At work, Farrah had a different kind of relationship with men, where they treated her well and with respect. Farrah started to look at factors that encouraged this kind of relationship and identified two large themes: (a) sharing a common project or goal with her co-workers, and (b) not having the relationships impacted by substance use. Specifically, neither she nor her co-workers were using substances on the job, which decreased incidences of abuse.

By completing this exercise, Farrah became increasingly motivated to change her drinking habits and restructure her support network that had previously consisted of heavy drinkers. Farrah realized that work had served as a refuge for her and that she acted differently on the job. She focused on feelings of being part of a team and being empowered and wrote down associated thoughts. Farrah was able to identify cues and behaviors that elicited support from others, along with articulating positive statements about herself, thus helping to improve her self-concept.

Exercise 3: Choices. Rice (2008) suggests reflecting on major life choices relative to traumatic events (past, current, and future-related), and how personal responsibility has or has not been accepted for each of these choices. A question posed to clients is: "How could you respond to any present difficulty in a way that would empower you?" (Rice, 2008, p. 119). The goal of this essay/composition exercise is for clients to re-evaluate beliefs of powerlessness or lack of control and to understand personal freedom and their responsibility to exercise that freedom.

Clinical example: *Damien was a handsome, 23-year-old college graduate with a traumatic brain injury. In the winter following graduation from college, he decided to go skiing with friends while intoxicated. It was a miracle Damian survived the ski accident, but the damage to his brain left him impulsive and argumentative. Damien struggled with his life post-accident, retreating to a world inside the house smoking cannabis. He experienced irritability and difficulty getting motivated. He was unable to keep a job for long and would often blow up at co-workers. Damien was referred for outpatient psychotherapy to help him with occupational and social difficulties.*

The work with Damien was slow and challenging. The initial stages were geared toward building up Damien's sense of personal agency.

> There was a great degree of denial about the impact his brain injury was having on his functioning. At the same time, many of his symptoms could not necessarily be solely attributed to the injury. Damien was depressed, and he was angry. Completing the exercise above on choices was part of a long segment of work focusing on the trauma of the accident.
>
> Damien experienced unresolved guilt and anger regarding the accident, having difficulty acknowledging his role in the accident and its consequences. This exercise was used toward the end of this portion of work, when Damien was able to express his role in the trauma. He grieved his choice to go skiing under the influence, which allowed him to acknowledge the choices available to him in the present. Indeed, for him to move forward he needed to fully accept what had occurred and the role he played.
>
> Damien began to see that his current behavior was perpetuating a pattern of denying responsibility for himself. He started to see that using substances had only brought suffering for him and others. Slowly, Damien began reducing his cannabis use, which had exacerbated the effects of his brain injury. As he experienced success with this and increased motivation, he saw that he was better able to control his emotional outbursts. He also felt capable of starting a new job search in earnest, one of his major goals.

Exercise 4: Holding Opposites. The following exercise may help clients further grasp dialectics or increase their ability to mentally hold opposing ideas. "Irreconcilable opposites do not exist; opposing attitudes and methods can be united in a constructive synthesis. The matter could be formulated also in this way: it is not "this or that," but "this *and* that" (Assagioli, 1967, p. 12). Clients may start by writing one central thought or emotion related to the trauma, followed by something that may seem contradictory or opposed to the original thought or emotion. For example, an opening sentence might read, "I was physically hurt during the rape, AND I am still physically able to enjoy sex." Clients are then asked to finish an essay/composition that directly addresses the reasons for such a dichotomy, how well they can accept holding such opposite beliefs/emotions, and what this means to them. This exercise can also help explore seemingly contradictory or ambivalent feelings regarding the perpetrator, as well as any other aspects of the trauma and its effects.

> **Clinical example:** *Baker realized that his mother likely had Borderline Personality Disorder. He learned about the disorder through a previous therapist and felt that it resonated with his experience of his mother and of himself. Baker had expressed feelings of chronic emptiness and an interpersonal paranoia that was frequently dysregulating and disheartening. He was depressed and tried to cope with drugs, masturbation, and sexual "hook-ups" with men he met online.*

A large trigger for Baker was "black and white" thinking where he would become upset with someone and start to villainize him or her, while also thinking of himself in the worst possible terms. Therapeutic work incorporated the concept of dialectics from Dialectical Behavior Therapy. The exercise above fit nicely within that framework and was appropriate in helping Baker hold seemingly opposing ideas. He began to think of his relationships and himself differently, being able to contain anger and rage better.

Baker completed this exercise many times regarding different social situations and suicidality. He kept his reflections in a journal and was able to read his dialectical statements to challenge his polarized thinking when in crisis. He was able to accept more parts of himself and no longer saw himself as worthless or despicable. Writing down his "opposites" became a regular practice for Baker. He was able to record reflections on index cards to keep on his person during a hard day or to put in his coping tool kit where he kept phone numbers of his support system, as well as ideas for healthy ways to self-soothe.

Focus on Others

Exercise 5: Describing Traumatic Events to Different Audiences. Pennebaker (2004) suggests describing a traumatic event to different symbolic audiences with the idea that our writing compositions will change in tone, focus, word choice, and perhaps even extent of disclosure based on our intended audience. This essay/composition exercise is intended to help clients perceive the many ways in which trauma events can be described and how we must often censor, adjust, or otherwise change these descriptions based on the demands of different audiences. The hope is that at the end of such an essay writing exercise, clients will be able to see that there is no singular "right way" to describe trauma events. Instead, descriptions of trauma are almost always adjusted to the social norms inherent within distinct groups of people. We suggest that therapists use the following script to begin this exercise with clients:

> For this exercise, you will be writing to four entirely different individuals about the same traumatic event. The exercise should take about 40 minutes, with 10 minutes spent writing to each one. The four people will be:
>
> - someone in authority
> - someone who was there during the event
> - a close friend
> - yourself
>
> Think of *someone in authority* over you, who you must convince that the traumatic event has deeply impacted you. Visualize this person, and write with him or her in mind. Take about 10 minutes to complete this portion of the essay.

Then, think about *someone who was present* during or immediately after the traumatic event, someone who has a very different view of what happened, or does not otherwise agree with your description of events. Take 10 minutes for this portion of the task.

Next, think about *a close friend* who accepts you without condition and without judgment. Describe to him or her how the trauma impacted you during and after the event. Take another 10 minutes to finish this section.

End the entire essay by writing for 10 minutes to *yourself* about the traumatic event. What were the most important things that happened? What were your thoughts and feelings, both during and after the event?

Afterwards, notice the difference in your feelings, thoughts, tones, and words used across the four different people. Were your feelings/thoughts different for each one? Was one harder to write than the others? If so, why? Did you come away with a different perspective on the effects of the trauma on you? If so, how?

Exercise 6: Developing Compassion. The following may help assist clients with writing a perspective-taking essay/composition in regard to the trauma in their lives. They are asked to imagine their own struggles as if they were happening to someone else, helping them develop compassion for themselves and how others might cope with what they are going through. We suggest the following therapist script to help clients begin this exercise:

Place yourself mentally in a situation where someone you love has undergone a trauma—similar to yours or different. What would you be feeling? How would you approach this person or what might you say? Think about him or her developing similar symptoms or difficulties to your own. What would that be like for you and how might you treat this person? Would you try to deny what had happened to him or her, or maybe become overly care-taking or responsible? How would you be able to come to terms with what happened and the effects on your loved one? Pretend you're explaining what it is like for you now to know what has happened to him or her and to see how it is impacting his or her life. Write an essay about what it has been like for your loved one.

Clinical example: *Alma had an abortion last year and presented to treatment following a break-up with her boyfriend. She wondered if the abortion had taken a toll on the relationship but figured it was so early in the relationship that it was the right thing to do, especially since they were not in the right place in their lives to have a child together. Alma presented with euthymic mood and constricted affect. She reported irritability and a desire not to be bothered by the break-up with her ex.*

During therapy, it became clear that Alma had many unresolved feelings regarding the pregnancy and the abortion. She kept telling herself to shrug it off and move on, but became tearful when describing how the pregnancy felt and how it made her long for children with her then-partner. She appeared to have little tolerance for allowing herself to grieve and feel strong emotions regarding what had happened. The writing exercise, "Developing Compassion" allowed her to imagine how she would act if something similar had happened to a loved one.

When Alma imagined what she would feel or say if her close friend also had an abortion, she respected the sense of loss her friend would experience. She certainly wouldn't just expect her friend to "get over it", and would understand the vulnerability her friend might have experienced under similar circumstances. The different perspective-taking prompted by this exercise allowed Alma to develop more compassion for herself and her struggle—something that didn't come to her naturally as she had high expectations of herself regarding her ability to manage emotions and "pull it together."

Exercise 7: Forgiving Others. Writing an essay or composition about forgiveness might be helpful because it is often a difficult topic to broach and may take years or decades for trauma survivors to think in terms of forgiving a perpetrator (Pennebaker, 2004). Many confuse forgiveness for condoning the wrongdoings or violence committed by another. Rather, forgiveness can be viewed as releasing anger or resentment held toward another so that energy can be reinvested in one's life and healing may occur. Here is a suggested therapist script to use when beginning such a writing exercise:

> Think about a situation in which you were treated very badly by someone else, resulting in hurt or suffering. Recall what happened before, during, and after the specific event and how you felt. Recall the event in as much detail as possible. Take about five minutes to describe the event.
>
> Afterwards, write about your emotions and thoughts about the situation for approximately 10 minutes and how it has affected you. Then, switch focus to the individual who hurt you. What could he or she have been thinking? Feeling? What could have made him or her believe that hurting you was the best thing to do at that moment? What was going on in his or her life at the time? If he or she were here, what do you think he or she would say about the reasons for hurting you? Does he or she have awareness of how the situation hurt you (or not)?
>
> Take yet another 10 minutes to complete this essay from the other's perspective. Write in an open and honest way, then ask yourself what it would take to release the anger and hurt that the person caused. If the person must make amends in order for you to forgive, what are the chances he or she would be willing to do so? What will you do if

you're sure this person will never make amends? How will you cope with this knowledge? What are the positives and negatives of forgiving anyway? Not forgiving? If you were to forgive, what would it look like? How will you know when you have forgiven (or not)?

Clinical example: *Jeremy was a successful businessman in his 40s who had a history of physical and emotional abuse by his father. He grew up in several different towns in what he termed, "the slums" due to his father's erratic job history and aggressive behavior. Jeremy described how his father would become combative with landlords and neighbors. His violent streak was even more pronounced at home where Jeremy would get beaten by his father if he "looked at him the wrong way." Many years had passed and Jeremy had a strained and distant relationship with his father. As soon as he moved out of the house, he only spoke to his father when absolutely necessary, usually just to request financial assistance during difficult years earning his educational degrees after high school.*

Although his father seemed to "mellow" with age, Jeremy never forgot the horrifying experience growing up at home with him. He felt constantly as if he was walking on egg shells around his father, and struggled with body image and identity issues from pre-puberty through young adulthood. Although Jeremy made vast improvements in therapy regarding chronic suicidality and depression, he still struggled with irritability and anger. He was a spiritual person who used his own spiritual practice to help cope with these issues with some success. However, the deep-seated anger toward his father often drained his emotional energy and prevented him from moving forward. Even though he barely spoke to him, the fact that his father was still alive disturbed him.

Treatment began to focus on issues of forgiveness and what that would mean for Jeremy's recovery. Jeremy completed the "Forgiving Others" exercise to begin the lengthy process of reclaiming some of the psychic energy that had previously been invested in hatred toward his father. He picked several particularly traumatic events and completed the exercise for each of them. It took him several writing attempts to achieve a deeper resolution to the issue of forgiveness, especially given the extent and longevity of abuse. The exercise not only served as exposure to the traumatic memories, but was truly integrated into the concept of forgiveness that proved deeply meaningful to Jeremy in terms of growing in his spiritual practice.

As Jeremy wrote about his past abuse, he began to realize the pervasiveness and gravity of his father's undiagnosed mental illness. He also realized that his father would never be able to recognize or take responsibility for how he acted during those years. These realizations facilitated Jeremy's grieving process, and finally allowed him to release much of the anger and hatred he had been holding on to. It just didn't make sense anymore for Jeremy to own the pain and resentment resulting from having his life affected by this man who was so ill and unaware of the damage he had done. Jeremy began to understand that much of his irritability and anger stemmed from a sense of loss and really being an orphan for many years.

Exercise 8: Asking for Forgiveness. In life, most of us are aware of situations in which we have caused suffering in another. Because no one is immune to causing others suffering in some way (even if only in minor ways), this exercise can be paired with the one immediately above. Once again, asking for forgiveness does not mean excusing or agreeing with our own hurtful behavior. Asking for forgiveness from others as a writing exercise can allow clients to see the other side of a hurtful situation with more clarity. Here are suggested instructions for completing such a writing task:

> Think about a situation in which you treated someone else badly, resulting in hurt or suffering. Recall what happened before, during, and after the specific event and how you felt and what you were thinking. Recall the event in as much detail as possible. Take about five minutes to describe the event.
>
> Afterwards, write about your emotions and thoughts about the situation for approximately 10 minutes and how it affected you. Don't use this to justify your actions; instead, write about your motivations, emotions, and thoughts in that moment. Then, switch focus to the individual who you hurt. What could he or she have been thinking? Feeling? If he or she were here, what do you think he or she would say about the effects of your hurtful actions on him or her, family, or friends? Did this person know why you hurt him or her?
>
> Take yet another 10 minutes to complete this writing task from the other's perspective. Write in an open and honest way, then ask yourself what it would take to make amends for the hurt you caused. Exactly what would you do and say to apologize or make amends? Imagine if the person were here: would he or she be willing to hear an apology from you? Why or why not? What would the response be should you try to make amends? Are you willing to do those things? What will you do if you're sure your apology will never be accepted? How would you cope with this knowledge? What are the positives and negatives of apologizing or making amends anyway?

Part III-IV
Free-Writing Exercises

We have chosen to place this section at the end because the two exercises presented here are the least structured of all. They can be used throughout the therapy process, whenever a client seems "stuck" or cannot think of material to complete specific assignments.

Exercise 1: Semiautomatic Writing. Often, when writing we tend to self-sensor. This exercise is meant to help break through this tendency. It should be noted, however, that this exercise may not be suited for clients with thought disorders, those who are disorganized, or those who have not built up safety and coping skills. It may further exacerbate a lack of cognitive or emotional organization, and more structured exercises (e.g., sentence stems) might be better suited for individuals exhibiting these traits. The following is a suggested therapist script intended to help clients engage in semiautomatic writing:

> This type of writing exercise is used to help break through the tendency to censor ourselves. The one central rule to this exercise is to *not* look at your hands while writing, or what you are producing while writing. This means that if you are writing by hand, you must look away from your writing surface during the exercise; if writing by computer, you must look away from the keyboard and screen. If you find you cannot keep from looking, you might try using a towel to cover your hand and the writing surface or the computer screen and keyboard; just make sure not to block your hand while writing or typing. You should also expect that if writing by hand, you will make writing mistakes and not be able to stay within the lines. If writing by computer, you should expect many typos. None of this matters. The main idea is to simply write whatever comes to mind without worry.
>
> Next, distract yourself. Look out the window, or gaze at your feet. Write without direction or purpose; write whatever comes up for you. Try to write this way for five minutes, and with practice increase in length to 10 minutes. Then take a look at what you have written. It may surprise you!

Exercise 2: Into the Stream. It is often helpful to increase clients' abilities to conduct the passive observation of physical sensations, thoughts, and emotions. To increase such skills, clients may respond to the question: "What's going on for you right now, in this moment?" (Adams, 1998, p. 20). A writing exercise that can tap into this process is "stream of consciousness" writing. Pennebaker (2004, pg. 62) provides a writing exercise that helps the individual practice observing the stream of consciousness by using the following instructions: "… write in a stream of consciousness manner for ten minutes or until two [blank] pages are filled. As you write, simply track your thoughts and feelings as they [arise] … [and write down] what you are feeling, hearing, smelling, or noticing. It is important [to simply] follow your stream of thought. Don't worry about spelling, grammar, or sentence structure … just begin writing and don't stop."

Part III-V
Activity-Based Exercises

As adjuncts to writing exercises, we've found it important to be knowledgeable about other types of therapeutic activities that are useful in trauma work. In this section, we present a series of relaxation exercises, imagery exercises, and multi-media exercises. Relaxation exercises may help clients deal with intense thoughts and emotions before or after engaging with earlier writing exercises that explicitly target trauma-related material. Similarly, imagery exercises can also help in coping with intense thoughts and emotions, and may also assist in jump-starting a client's creative processes. Multi-media exercises are intended to broaden the healing mechanisms inherent within creative activities by bringing in other types of artistic endeavors when dealing with trauma. All three types of exercises can be utilized at various points throughout therapy, whenever the therapist or client deems them helpful.

Section 1: Relaxation Exercises

Exercise 1: Diaphragmatic Breathing. Therapists often coach clients through diaphragmatic breathing, with many different recommendations available in the literature (e.g., Curran, 2010). We offer the following therapist script:

> Close your eyes. Now place one hand on your chest and the other on your lower belly. Take a deep breath and let it out. Take another until the hand on your belly expands out farther than the hand on your chest. When your belly expands farther than your chest, you know your diaphragm is bringing air deep into your lower lungs.
>
> Take another deep breath, this time through your nose. Take in as much air as you can. Hold it for a count of 5. Now exhale through your mouth for a count of 8. As you exhale, release into relaxation. At the end, gently contract your belly muscles to expel as much air as you can. This way, you will deepen your breathing by completely expelling the air in your lungs, not by taking more in.
>
> Breathe in through your nose and exhale through your mouth 4 more times. Try to breathe in and out once about every 12 seconds. At this rate you might notice your heart beat will increase and decrease as you inhale and exhale. This can have a positive effect on cardiac health.

In general, you should exhale about twice as long as you inhale, and your belly should expand more than your chest with each inhale. Once you are comfortable with breathing from your belly and the timing of each breathing cycle, you will no longer need to monitor your breathing with your hands.

Exercise 2: Progressive Muscle Relaxation (PMR). Again, therapists often coach clients through progressive muscle relaxation (PMR), with many different recommendations available in the literature (e.g., Curran, 2010). Some offer kinesthetic focus from the top of the body (head) to the bottom (feet), while others reverse the focus (bottom to top). We suggest using the following therapist script that moves from the feet to the head:

> Sit in the chair with your feet flat on the floor and your hands flat on the armrests. Sit up straight and get comfortable while relaxing into the seat of the chair. Feel the soles of your feet flat on the floor. Feel the palms of your hands flat on the armrests. Feel the back of your thighs against the seat of the chair. Slowly close your eyes and take a deep breath, then slowly exhale.
>
> Begin by tensing all the muscles in your feet. Scrunch up your toes and make the tops of your feet and your ankles rigid. Inhale and hold for a count of 4. As you exhale, slowly release the tension in your toes, feet, and ankles. Now exhale and relax completely. Let your toes, feet, and ankles go completely lax, as though they were jelly. Feel the tension flow from your feet right into the floor. Enjoy the feeling.
>
> Next, completely tense your calf muscles and knees by pointing your feet and extending your legs, again inhaling and counting to 4. Then exhale and relax. Feel the tension go from your knees, through your calves and feet, straight into the floor.
>
> Continue up the body, repeating the procedure by tensing and relaxing the following muscle groups:
>
> - thighs (pretend you are pressing a penny between your knees)
> - buttocks
> - lower belly and back
> - chest and upper back (extend both arms and clench your fists)
> - biceps of both arms
> - both forearms and hands (making a fist)
> - shoulders and neck (raise your shoulders up to your ears; point your chin down toward chest and/or up toward the ceiling)
> - face and scalp
>
> Once you have finished with the face and scalp, tense the entire body for a count of 3 while taking a deep breath. Finish by exhaling deeply and letting all tension from your entire body flow down and out

through the feet and into the floor. Take one more deep breath, inhale then exhale. Now check for any signs of tension within your whole body. You should now be completely relaxed.

Take note of any residual tension. Note where in the body you seem to be holding the most rigid tension. You may now wish to repeat the procedure in any location still holding tension until you are completely relaxed.

Following PMR, clients can write responses to the following questions: What does this exercise bring to mind? Does what you just experienced remind you of another time in your life when you experienced relaxation? What emotions come up from this activity?

Section 2: Guided Imagery

Adams (1998) suggests following guided visualizations with written reflection about feelings and thoughts that arose and what they may be saying about waking life. Additionally, she advises clients to write about guided imagery in the present tense to reflect the visualization's nearness to the present and its continued energy in clients' lives. Lastly, Adams notes clients may write a list of questions raised by the visualization, then go back to answer the questions. Any of the following visualizations may be followed by a written reflection answering these questions:

- What images, thoughts, and feelings arose?
- What was the most powerful feeling?
- On a scale of 1 to 10, from low to high intensity, how intense was this feeling?
- If this feeling were a physical sensation what would it be?
- What is this experience telling me?

Exercise 1: Safety-centering. Clients imagine their "safe place" when beginning a writing session or feeling overwhelmed.[2] The following dialogue may be initiated by the therapist right before the writing exercise begins:

> Now let us turn to centering on feelings of peace and safety before beginning the writing exercise for this session. Which place would you like to imagine where you have felt a strong sense of peace and safety? (Therapist may suggest a "safe place" that was previously mentioned or written about by the client). Mentally focus yourself on this place. You may close your eyes if you are comfortable doing so. What does it feel like to be in this place? What do you see, smell, and hear? What

---

[2] This is similar to Adams's (1998) idea that it is often beneficial to start writing sessions with an initial meditation to quiet the mind.

do you see yourself doing? Relax into this place for a few moments. Take a few slow, deep breaths. How do you feel now? (Note: insure that client reports being in a more relaxed state, then proceed to the chosen writing exercise.)

Exercise 2: Visualizing Emotional Symbols. Visualization techniques help clients explore their own awareness of emotions by envisioning symbols of selected affective states. For example, the color blue can induce a tranquilizing effect where clients may visualize themselves at the center of a globe filled with a given color in a scene or object with a particular color (e.g., blue bird; Gerard, 1961).

Exercise 3: Doorway to Feeling. According to Gerard (1961), clients may be asked to imagine a door with a particular feeling word written on it (e.g., anxiety, love, hate) then open the door and report who or what they encounter on the other side.

> **Clinical example:** *Gary grew up with a rageful, alcoholic father and was anticipating the birth of his first child. Treatment had focused on his continued relationship with his father, who was now aging and still struggling with alcoholism. Gary's abuse history was also impacting his current relationship with his wife, and he was often feeling taxed in the marriage as he struggled with the current relationship with his father and the ghosts of his father's past abusive behavior.*
>
> *Gary came to treatment feeling stressed and anxious about the future, worrying about the role he wanted his father to play as a grandparent and about potentially needing to support his father in his old age. He felt ambivalent about this relationship, and conversations with his father had been impacting his mood, placing further strain on his marital interactions. After completing the "Safety-centering" exercise noted above, Gary was guided through the meditation exercise, "Doorway to Feeling." He imagined a door with the word "anxiety" written on it and was able to experience a fruitful reflection on what lay beyond this door after it opened. Gary wrote quickly on what insights he obtained through this guided imagery. His writing revealed grief over the loss of a healthy father-son relationship growing up. However, one of the fears most surprising to Gary was the fear of being abusive like his father to his soon-to-be-born son. Gary's writing served as a springboard for therapeutic discussion and helped accelerate Gary's treatment progress.*

Exercise 4: Getting to the Heart of the Matter. Clients can visualize a huge heart that is bigger than themselves (eight to 10 feet high) and enter it through a door—Where is the door located? Where does it lead? Is anyone there? According to Gerard (1961), this exercise will help clients explore deeper emotions and associated symbolic images.

Exercise 5: Meeting with You Again. The following questions are aimed at facilitating grieving. The following questions are excerpted and modified from the AIDS Poetry Project Workbook 2 (1997, as cited in Mazza, 1999, p. 181):

> Pretend that you are in your bed, thinking of [the person you have lost] and suddenly you feel his or her comforting presence in the room. What is this like? How do you recognize that it is his or her presence? How do you feel? What do you learn from the experience?

Additional questions can be added to this exercise. Based on work by Gerard (1961), we suggest that clients be asked to engage in further visualizations and elaborations:

> What do they look like? What is communicated between the two of you? How do you feel about what has been communicated? What thoughts come to mind?

> **Clinical example:** *Cora's fiancé was shot and killed in a gang-related street fight when he was in the wrong place at the wrong time. She had gone into a convenience market to quickly pick something up, only to hear gun shots close to where he was waiting outside. Subsequently, she experienced a devastating depression and intrusive thoughts about the event.*
>
> *Cora's entire life was put on hold, and other than going to work, she retreated into social isolation while experiencing hours of dissociation. Cora was experiencing a great deal of emotional numbing, and this exercise helped reconnect her with her grief. She imagined her fiancé's presence and imagined a dialogue with him. Cora completed this exercise many times and wrote down her reflections. Doing so helped her resolve the trauma of this abruptly truncated relationship with someone with whom she intended to spend the rest of her life.*
>
> *Although Cora was initially skeptical, she began to understand the wisdom and strength offered by the memory of her fiancé. She realized he didn't want her to be unhappy and to suffer. In her own way, letting him go and moving forward with her life would serve as her gift to him, as well as a lasting expression of her love. She understood that she would rather be the one to survive him and to spare him the pain she had been experiencing. This gave her a renewed sense of meaning in her life, and she was able to re-engage socially and with work.*

Exercise 6: Unifying Centers. Gerard (1961) suggests imagining symbols of "unifying centers" that may resolve a client's personality conflicts. When trauma disrupts one's sense of self or leads to split-off and dissociated parts of the personality, such visualizations may help clients access a more grounded place. Gerard (1961) suggests clients imagine reaching a lighthouse on a rock after a dangerous swim in a choppy ocean, then ascending the lighthouse to look at the ocean. This visualization may also be helpful in developing "wise mind," and creating balance between rational and emotional thinking (Linehan, 1993). Continuing this exercise, clients then imagine what they observe while swimming through the churning waters, to gain understanding about the conflicts they are experiencing. Much like the concept of experiential liberation, clients are supported in "re-occupying" or embodying the parts of themselves that have been denied (Schneider, 2008).

Exercise 7: Mirroring Change. Certain visualizations can suggest inevitable changes, such as a chrysalis changing to a butterfly, a closed rosebud opening up and growing into a full-grown rose (very gradually, as nature grows), or a seed growing into a tree (Gerard, 1961). Asking clients to visualize current problems as issues that will inevitably change can help them in the process of growth and inner development, as well as accessing and initiating their internal creative process (Gerard, 1961).

Exercise 8: My Ideal Activities and Behaviors. Clients may envision acquiring a particular personality characteristic symbolically. For example, a client who would like a sense of inner peace can imagine a stormy ocean that becomes still and calm. Gerard (1961) suggests a few visualizations for this type of exercise, such as imagining undoing a tangled knot for the desired characteristic of patience, waking from a slumber to clear perception of a situation as a characteristic of sudden clarity, or taming and training a wild horse as a simile for getting emotional swings under control. Clients may then envision all the activities they wish they could engage in, along with desired behaviors associated with them.

> **Clinical example:** *Eli was mugged late one night when walking home from his college classes. Since that time, he used alcohol and marijuana heavily. His grades began to slip, and he came in for psychotherapy. Initial work focused on engagement and his goals. As a result of intrusive traumatic memories and inattentiveness, he was finding it hard to complete classroom assignments. One of Eli's major complaints was his difficulty with attention. He was starting to panic about his academic performance, and his major goal was to work on his attention issues.*
>
> *The above exercise, "My Ideal Activities and Behaviors," served to focus the treatment and helped enhance Eli's feelings of confidence and hope regarding change. He imagined a swarming buzz of bees surrounding him that suddenly dissipated, opening to a calm, clear lake under a sunny sky. He imagined constructing a small building by this lakeside that had a large, clean, organized desk facing a bright, open window overlooking the lake. Eli imagined himself successfully*

and productively working through many assignments that had been postponed. He really entered into the experience of imagining himself performing to high potential, vigorously and efficiently focusing on each task with calm and confidence.

Eli then wrote out this reflection, focusing especially on the feelings of calm and confidence. The office by the lake served as a visual cue to evoke these feelings. He also noticed characteristics of the scene that loaned themselves to high levels of productivity, including a quiet and organized work space. Eli then crafted a plan of how to create and ensure these characteristics for a stable, consistent workplace in the real world.

Exercise 9: Visualizing a Traumatic Memory. Clients are asked to visualize one of the first images that come to mind regarding a traumatic memory. The following questions may then be asked:

- What are the physical sensations you experience when you contemplate this (object, scene, event)?
- What kind of thoughts, feelings, and impressions come up?
- Which of these thoughts are no longer useful to you in how you want to live your life?

Exercise 10: Imagining a Different Outcome. Extending the above imagery exercise, clients are asked to repeatedly imagine a distressing traumatic scene where each time the outcome is improved.

Exercise 11: A Reflection of Myself. In order to uncover beliefs about one's self, as well as thoughts related to self-image, clients may imagine entering a room and looking into a mirror, or going into a garden and looking at their reflection in a pool (Gerard, 1961).

Exercise 12: Reconstructing the Self. When clients are dealing with a sense of being damaged or broken by trauma in their lives, it may be helpful to actively visualize reconstructive images such as building an intact, beautiful, strong home or temple to replace a dilapidated house (Gerard, 1961). Gerard offers the additional image of restoring a garden and suggests picturing its growth in beauty for a few minutes day after day until the client can fully imagine its beauty.

Exercise 13: Body Sensations as Images. Clients can visualize somatic states with accompanying images and physiological sensations (Gerard, 1961). An example of this might be if a client reports a sick feeling in the stomach. The therapist might guide the client to close his or her eyes, sit with the sensation, and then describe it in detail. The therapist might then ask if any images come to mind while the client is sitting with the stomach sensation.

Exercise 14: My Body as Myself. Clients explore how their bodies are linked to how they define themselves before and after trauma. Questions to help begin this imagery exercise are:

- What messages were given to you about your body?
- Were there any other implicit messages you received about your body?
- Now visualize your body, as if looking at yourself in a full-length mirror.
- Where have these messages lodged in your body?

Suggested messages to use as examples might be: "Your body is respected, *unless* you push my buttons or I get angry," or "Your body is ugly and you should try harder at making it perfect/pleasing to others."

Exercise 15: Healing Colors. Similar to visualizing colors associated with emotion, Comas-Diaz (2008) suggests that clients focus on a color they associate with healing and then imagine these colors in a scene where they are flowing through one's body. Alternatively, clients can visualize healing colors that are concentrated within a particularly problematic body part or general area.

Exercise 16: Conflict-focused Visualizations. Clients may visualize people with whom they have experienced or are experiencing conflict (Gerard, 1961). For example, a man who is fighting with his family regarding their lack of acceptance regarding his assault victimization, might imagine a more open, desired dialogue with his family members. This exercise is salient when working on mistrust of others as a result of trauma (Foa et al., 1999; Harris & Valentiner, 2002).

Exercise 17: Images of Integration and Balance. Gerard (1961) suggests visualizing images associated with integration and balance (such as visualizing a sunflower's symmetry), as well as symbols that center on harmonious human relations (hands clasping). Visualizing and then meditating on these images may bring up powerful feelings related to the concepts of inner balance or human relationships. Regarding interpersonal recovery after trauma, it may be useful to introduce images that focus on collaboration between individuals, such as visualizing walking on a path with another person and helping one another surmount obstacles.

Exercise 18: Images of Light. Clients may visualize light as a metaphor for self-understanding and insight (Gerard, 1961). Clients imagine approaching, then entering a flaming sphere, shining diamond, radiating star, or sun (Gerard, 1961) and are asked:

- What do you see?
- How does that feel within your body?
- What thoughts come to mind?
- What feelings do you notice?

Section 3: Multimedia Activities

Exercise 1: Music Reflection. Clients may listen to any passage of music and share their emotional reaction (Assagioli, 1967). They are asked to attend to, identify, and note their inner states and feelings.

Exercise 2: Expressing Feelings through Art. When incorporating other modes of artistic expression to identify and label strong feelings, clients may draw, paint, or create a collage (e.g., photography or pictures from a magazine) that best represents the selected emotion (Adams, 1998).

> **Clinical example:** *Janine, 49-years-old, had had other therapists in the past, all who treated her chronic depression. Her most recent therapist abruptly left the center a few weeks prior to her beginning psychotherapy with me, and we discussed how difficult it was for her to make this transition to another therapist. Janine grew up in an alcoholic family, her father raging against her and her brother. Our work initially began with the loss of her prior therapist, and progressed to discussing the loss of care-taking growing up.*
>
> *As the end to our work approached, Janine showed immense resilience and was receptive to creating artwork as part of her termination. She handcrafted a beautifully made card out of cardboard as a way of saying good-bye to me and a way of symbolically commemorating our work together. She took time to cut cardboard to a smaller, square size and used markers, glue, and glitter to decorate the inside and outside of the card. Filling the entire front of the card was a large rainbow, richly colored by markers with silvery glitter. She then drew flowers around the inside with fine-tipped markers. Her writing was simple and touching and included poetry that resonated with her for the occasion of saying goodbye. Her artwork was a symbol of the work we had done, the space in which she could express grief and have her pain acknowledged. She had changed in the process of therapy and showed that in this artistic, symbolic creation.*

Exercise 3: Role-plays Using Parts of the Self. Clients role-play, or act out a part of themselves that they generally suppress in everyday life (Schneider, 2008). Therapists can help get clients started by asking:

- Who is that person?
- How does that part talk and walk?
- What does he or she believe?
- After the role play, what did that feel like?
- How much did you resist it?
- How much did you feel freed by the experience?
- What did all of this mean to you?

Exercise 4: Acting out a Different Outcome. Clients create a script and act out different roles that create new possibilities and/or different outcomes to traumatic events. This can help to engage the body in reorganizing memories of the trauma (Rothschild, 2000).

Exercise 5: Trauma Objects. Research has shown that exposure to painful reminders of trauma is often beneficial for people who have experienced trauma (Foa et al., 2002; Foa & Kozak, 1986, as cited in Pennebaker, 2004; Foa & Rothbaum, 1998), even though trauma survivors may have a great deal of anxiety surrounding trauma-related triggers (e.g., certain holidays, social settings, volume of the vocal expression of others, and so on). Sometimes, they may even be unaware of what causes them a great deal of anxiety or thrusts them into a state of fight or flight. It is the job of the therapists and clients to identify these triggers. If clients have completed some of the exercises in this workbook (particularly the imaginal exposure exercises), they likely have awareness of many of their trauma-related triggers. In the vein of exposure therapy, clients may choose to have with them symbols or tangible objects reminding them of trauma during the exercise below. The following therapist script may be particularly helpful as an introduction to *in-vivo* exposure:

> Please recall a traumatic event in your life. Recall the place, the situation, the people, even the furniture, clothing, or smells that were present. The idea is to create a list of the strongest reminders or symbols of the traumatic event. This could include just about anything, from the time of day or night, the tone or loudness of someone's voice, to letters or pictures, whatever is associated with the event. Once you have created a list of the top three items, do the following:
>
> - Take a moment to look over your list. If there are things on your list that you possess (e.g., something concrete such as a letter or a newspaper clipping), please place them in front of you so that you can handle them, even smell them. If there are things on your list that can only be recalled from memory, then actively remember them. Do this in order of the items on your list.

- While handling each concrete thing you possess associated with the trauma, or recall from memory the strongest reminders, note some of the sensations, emotions, and thoughts each of these has for you, in order of your list.

Exercise 6: Confronting Trauma Triggers. For further desensitization, clients may create a hierarchy of trauma-related triggers that involve persons, places, and things that they then will encounter *in vivo*, or in real life. For someone who is a combat veteran, it could be loud noises. Given this hypothetical trigger, the client will purposefully expose him- or herself to this trigger and then reflect on the experience through writing. In order to have corrective experiences, clients will first need to identify and list trauma-related triggers (e.g., being outdoors, starting a romantic relationship) in order of how much anxiety these triggers provoke, then expose themselves to the anxiety-provoking stimuli; clients might then journal about their exposure experiences in order to share with the therapist or others (Bowen & Lambert, 1986).

Exercise 7: Mirror Reflection—Writing Exercise. Pennebaker (2004) cites research by Wicklund (1979) suggesting that people who are in front of a mirror tend to be more honest and aware of themselves. Based on this concept, Pennebaker (2004) suggests that writing in front of a mirror can be a powerful way of helping individuals self-reflect. Such an exercise may also elicit clients' feelings and beliefs about their bodies in the aftermath of trauma. This is relevant for human-perpetrated traumas, as well as natural disasters. Feelings of vulnerability surrounding one's body, as well as the greater issue of mortality may arise. The exercise is detailed below:

- For this writing exercise, it is best to find a place where your writing surface is next to a full-length mirror so that you can write while being able to see your entire body. If you do not have a full-length mirror, a hand-held mirror that is propped up next to your writing surface can be used, as long as you can see your entire face and head. Make sure you can see your own face and look directly into your own eyes before you begin this writing exercise.
- Next, look directly at yourself in the mirror, and notice your entire body (if you can), with special attention to your own eyes. While looking at yourself, think about the significant events in your life, and pick one that has had the most impact.
- After closely gazing at yourself in the mirror, write continuously for about 15 minutes, noting whatever comes to mind. Every once in a while, look back at yourself, especially gazing directly into your own eyes. Be honest, open, and free-flowing in your writing.

- How has the event shaped who you are? How you relate to others? How you view yourself? Who you have become?

> **Clinical example:** *Brigit was emotionally and physically abused by her mother growing up. There was a pervasive sense in the household that she was the identified "black sheep" and often found her siblings being given preferential treatment. She presented to treatment with suicidal thoughts and a great deal of self-loathing. Brigit's suicidal thoughts were examined and were often triggered by feelings of being disgusting and not good enough. She expressed deep-seated unhappiness with her body and was frequently preoccupied with perceived imperfections. Brigit admitted she had even begun avoiding looking at herself in the mirror to stave off self-critical and suicidal thoughts.*
>
> *The "Mirror Reflection—Writing Exercise" was employed to target these issues, and to work through a heightened sense of anxiety regarding body image through the use of the mirror. Brigit sat beside a full-length mirror for the exercise. She spent some moments looking thoroughly at her body, face, and eyes before she began writing. Throughout writing about her past and self-image, she returned to the mirror to periodically look at her body and face.*
>
> *By completing these exercises, Brigit's writing helped her to see that her mother's treatment affected how she saw herself as a woman and as a loveable person. Her chronic abuse history made her feel like she was unacceptable and tainted in some way. She realized she had begun to focus on her imperfections as a way to motivate herself toward self-improvement, yet also, as a means to feel close to her internalized, abusive mother who was now far away. She was able to move forward in treatment regarding grief over her mother and accepting herself in a more balanced way. She understood the internal dialogue of self-abuse was a remnant of the past and a way to keep her mother around. Her writing also helped Brigit to understand that she no longer needed this narrative to move forward and that change was necessary.*

Exercise 8: Engaging the Body through Drawing, Painting, Sculpting. It is said that the body holds the physiological and psychological impact of the trauma (Rothschild, 2000; Streeck-Fischer & van der Kolk, 2000; van der Kolk & Courtois, 2005). For this reason, it can be healing to further engage the body along with language-based components of writing and talking. Engagement of the body can be achieved through artistic mediums such as drawing, painting, and sculpting. Although the following exercise may be applied with a variety of artistic mediums, the instructions here are based on drawing to express feelings then writing about the artwork:

There are two basic types of this drawing exercise:
- free drawing, and
- drawing one's own body.

For the first exercise, you will need a few pieces of blank paper and a comfortable drawing surface. You can use pencils or pens; the idea is to create a free-flowing drawing of whatever comes to mind. It doesn't matter if you are a good drawer; even doodles or a series of circles would be fine. Once you have blank paper and drawing utensils ready, draw whatever is the first thing that you think of; just let your pencil or pen do the work. Don't erase or scratch out. Leave everything you have marked on the paper for later. Draw without stopping and across pages until you come to a natural stopping point. Free yourself to go as long as you like. After about 15 minutes or you've reaching a natural stopping point, examine your drawing. Then recall your feelings and thoughts, even body sensations, as you were drawing. Now spend another few minutes or so thinking about your drawing experience, making sure to dwell on any feelings or thoughts you had, as well as the experience of drawing. Were you aware of your hand across the page? Emotions or feelings? Did you know where the drawing was going, or did you surprise yourself?

For the second exercise, you will need the same materials. This time, however, you will draw a picture of your own body. Once again, it doesn't matter if you have drawing skill, or draw doodles, circles, or stick figures; all are just fine as long as you draw freely. Draw for about 15 minutes or you reach a natural stopping point. Now examine your drawing. As before, recall your feelings and thoughts, even body sensations, as you were drawing. Now spend another few minutes or so thinking about the experience of drawing your own body, making sure to dwell on any feelings or thoughts you had. Were you aware of your hand across the page? Emotions or feelings? Did you know where the drawing was going, or did you surprise yourself?

Part III-VI
Outcome Measures

Rationale

Measurements below will assist in determining whether treatment is effective for clients. Two areas of measurement include (a) improvement of post-traumatic stress symptoms, and (b) how the client perceives the therapeutic relationship throughout the process.

Screen for Post-traumatic Stress Symptoms (SPTSS)

The Screen for Post-traumatic Stress Symptoms (SPTSS, Carlson, 2001) is a brief screen for PTSD symptoms not based on a single-reported trauma, and is useful to assess those with possible multiple traumas, those who do not disclose past trauma, or those who have not been asked about past traumas. This is particularly important given that some people who endorse having experienced trauma on assessment screens do not develop PTSD. Conversely, those who answered "no" to having a trauma history may have indeed experienced traumatic stressors. Although exposure to trauma is generally associated with higher levels of post-traumatic stress symptoms, it does not always relate to PTSD symptom severity. Therefore, the SPTSS demonstrates a strength in that its evaluation of symptoms is not based on a single-reported trauma. Its brevity (three to five minutes to complete) and very low reading level make it an efficient and accessible instrument. It has been used with psychiatric inpatients, and has been found to have good reliability with internal consistency across items (Cronbach's alpha of .91), a high sensitivity rate in identifying clients with a PTSD diagnosis, and a moderate specificity rate in identifying clients without a PTSD diagnosis (ranging from .57 to .73). When compared to other trauma experience measures, SPTSS demonstrated good concurrent (correlations ranging from .68 to .79) and construct validity showing that the scale accurately measures post-traumatic symptomatology.

The Revised Helping Alliance Questionnaire (HAq-II)

The Revised Helping Alliance Questionnaire (HAq-II; Luborsky, Barber, Siqueland, Johnson, Najavits, Frank et al., 1996) assesses the relationship/rapport with therapist, which has been shown to be instrumental in treatment efficacy (Mulhauser, 2006). Results of this assessment can inform the clinician on alleviating problems with rapport, which may increase the efficacy of interventions. It was found to have excellent internal consistency and test-retest reliability, as well as high convergent validity with another measure of alliance.

Alternate Measures for the Assessment of Trauma Symptoms

Many measures would be useful in assessing the clinical picture of one who is suffering from post-traumatic stress. It appears that assessing various symptoms associated with post-traumatic stress is critical to gaining a broad view of the client's functioning and target areas for treatment. Some other measures that assess symptoms include: The Clinician-Administered Post-traumatic Stress Disorder Scale (CAPS-1, Blake, Weathers, Nagy, Kaloupek, Gusman, Charney, et al., 1995), the Post-traumatic Cognitions Inventory (PTCI, Foa, Ehlers, Clark, Tolin, & Orsillo, 1999), the Structured Interview for Disorders of Extreme Stress (SIDES, Pelcovitz, van der Kolk, Roth, Mandel, Kaplan, & Resick, 1997), and the Trauma and Attachment Belief Scale (TABS, Pearlman, 2003). All measures vary in scope of post-traumatic symptoms assessed, ease of use, reliability, and validity.

Strengths of the CAPS-1 include that it yields current (i.e., in the past month) and lifetime PTSD symptom scores, which helps provide a comprehensive picture of a client's functioning over time (Blake, Weathers, Nagy, Kaloupek, Gusman, Charney, et al., 1995). In addition, scores reveal disorder severity by rated frequency and intensity of symptoms, which can be useful in outcome studies. Although it requires training to administer, paraprofessionals can use the measure, which is beneficial when considering efficiency and resources. The scope of areas measured is comprehensive and includes associated symptoms, social and occupational functioning, improvement since last assessment, overall response validity, and overall PTSD severity.

In the CAPS-1, the addition of associated symptoms and social and occupational functioning are assets. However, associated symptoms were those found pertinent to combat veterans (e.g., survivor guilt, homicidality) and may not be generalizable across trauma survivors. Additional weaknesses include that the symptoms measured were modeled after DSM-III R criteria for PTSD and may reflect a more outdated diagnostic framework for PTSD. Overall, the CAPS-1 seems to be more of a diagnostic tool and may not be as relevant in monitoring treatment progress. Lastly, the interview seems lengthy, and a briefer self-report would be preferable for measuring post-traumatic stress symptoms periodically throughout treatment.

The SIDES is another structured interview designed to measure one's response to extreme stress on scales of alterations in regulation of affect and impulses, in attention or consciousness, in self-perception, in relations with others, somatization, and in systems of meaning (Pelcovitz, van der Kolk, Roth, Mandel, Kaplan, & Resick, 1997). A strength of the SIDES is that it provides a broader assessment of how trauma affects people in ways that are not captured by the diagnosis of PTSD, and can be useful in identifying areas of psychological impairment for treatment planning. Along with demonstration of inter-rater reliability, Zlotnick and Pearlstein (1997) found that SIDES showed adequate internal consistency and convergent validity as the SIDES scales correlated highly with instruments intended to measure similar constructs. Divergent validity was found for the following scales: alterations in regulation of affect and impulses, alterations in attention or consciousness, alterations in self-perception, and somatization. SIDES further demonstrated discriminant validity with minimal correlations found between SIDES subscales and a measure of narcissistic traits (Zlotnick & Pearlstein, 1997). However, a weakness is that SIDES may not be as efficient in tracking progress in symptom severity over the course of treatment as self-report measures that have more efficient administration. Lastly, it seems that more research on the measure's sensitivity and specificity needs to be conducted (Pelcovitz et al., 1997).

Other measures are more specific in the post-traumatic symptom domain that is explored. For example, the PTCI assesses negative cognitions about self, negative cognitions about the world, and self-blame (Foa, Ehlers, Clark, Tolin, & Orsillo, 1999). For this reason, this measure can be particularly useful in examining how the cognitive domain has been affected by trauma and can guide treatment regarding which area may be a particular focus. The PTCI has shown excellent internal consistency, good test-retest reliability, and construct validity demonstrated by moderate to high correlations with the Personal Beliefs and Reactions Scale (Resick et al., 1991 as cited in Foa et al., 1999). In addition, Foa and colleagues (1999) found discriminative validity in detecting differences between individuals with PTSD, traumatized individuals without PTSD, and non-traumatized individuals. Notably, the PTCI demonstrated good sensitivity and very high specificity by correctly classifying 86% of traumatized individuals into those with and without PTSD. However, this measure only assesses cognitions about self, world, and self-blame that have been affected by trauma, perhaps at the exclusion of other affected beliefs.

Similarly, TABS assesses how trauma affects one's belief system (Pearlman, 2003). These include beliefs about self and others in the five areas of safety, trust, esteem, intimacy, and control. A strength of TABS is that it can be used when the client doesn't meet diagnostic criteria for PTSD as it addresses other therapeutic problems—such as identifying disturbances in beliefs related to relational difficulties. Additionally, TABS can help document progress in treatment. Psychometrically, it has shown acceptable test-retest reliability and internal consistency, convergent and concurrent validity, discriminant validity demonstrated in nonclinical samples, sensitivity, and predictive and postdictive validity. Factorial validity has also been established (Ippen & Kulkarni, 2005; Varra, Pearlman, Brock, & Hodgson, 2008). A weakness of the scale is that it has been more widely used to measure vicarious traumatization rather than direct traumatization, and research is still needed to assess its usefulness with those who have directly experienced trauma. Lastly, caution is needed when interpreting TABS results for those with different cultural backgrounds, as differences in mean scores were found between different ethnic groups (Ippen & Kulkarni, 2005).

An overall downside to using the PTCI and TABS for assessment of initial and ongoing symptom severity is that they mainly focus on beliefs that have been affected by trauma. It seems that among measures of trauma symptomatology, there is variance in what trauma sequelae are examined. Therefore, broader measures of symptomatology, such as the SPTSS, would be better suited for this purpose.

Table 3.1 Measures for the Assessment of Trauma Symptoms

Measure	Symptoms Assessed	Ease of Use	Reliability	Validity
Clinician-Administered Posttraumatic Stress Disorder Scale (CAPS-1; Blake, Weathers, Nagy, Kaloupek, Gusman, Charney, et al., 1995)	DSM-informed symptoms of PTSD, associated symptoms, social and occupational functioning, improvement in PTSD symptoms since previous CAPS-1 assessment, overall response validity, and overall PTSD severity.	Structured interview that takes an average of 45 minutes with concise, standard prompt questions and behaviorally anchored rating scales. Scores for current and lifetime PTSD symptoms are produced. Requires training—can be used by clinicians and paraprofessionals.	Good inter-rater reliability, test-retest reliability for the three symptom clusters (.77–.96) and for all 17 items (.90–.98). Internal consistency for severity scores for three symptom clusters (α = .85–.87) and for all 17 items (α = .94).	Concurrent validity, good sensitivity (.84), and excellent specificity (.95). High convergent validity—total severity score correlated strongly with other measures of PTSD. High discriminant validity.
Posttraumatic Cognitions Inventory (PTCI; Foa, Ehlers, Clark, Tolin, & Orsillo, 1999)	Negative cognitions about self (e.g., permanent change, alienation, hopelessness, self-trust, and negative interpretation of symptoms), negative cognitions about the world (e.g., mistrust of other people), and self-blame.	33-item self-report; easy to understand and score with aid of scoring key.	Excellent internal consistency (α = .97) and good test-retest reliability (P = .74–.85).	Good convergent validity, construct validity, discriminative validity, and sensitivity. Very high specificity by correctly classifying 86% of trauma survivors into those with and without PTSD.

Measure	Symptoms Assessed	Ease of Use	Reliability	Validity
Screen for Posttraumatic Stress Symptoms (SPTSS; Carlson, 2001)	PTSD symptoms that closely match DSM-IV symptom criteria, but are not explicitly tied to a particular event.	Brief (3–5 min to complete), very low reading level (Flesch Grade Level of 7.5). Client must read 17 statements and assign a single rating to each on how frequently something has happened in the past two weeks. Scoring is the average of 17 items.	Good reliability, very good internal consistency across items (α = .91).	Good concurrent validity with other measures of PTSD (P = .68–.79) and construct validity. High sensitivity in identifying PTSD (.90–.95), and moderate specificity in identifying clients without PTSD diagnosis (.57–.73).
Structured Interview for Disorders of Extreme Stress (SIDES; Pelcovitz, van der Kolk, Roth, Mandel, Kaplan, & Resick, 1997) - (Zlotnick & Pearlstein, 1997)	Lifetime and current (i.e., past 6 months) alterations in regulation of affect and impulses, in attention or consciousness, in self-perception, in relations with others, somatization, and in systems of meaning.	48 items with severity ratings for symptoms on a 4-point scale ("none or no problem with symptom" to "extremely problematic"). Scoring involves the sum of severity ratings for each subscale.	Acceptable inter-rater reliability (κ = .81), acceptable internal consistency between scales (α = .53 to .96) and for the total SIDES score (α = .96).	Content and construct validity established. Convergent validity and high correlation with other measures of corresponding constructs. Divergent validity between scales.
Trauma and Attachment Belief Scale (TABS; Pearlman, 2003) - (Ippen & Kulkarni, 2005) - (Varra, Pearlman, Brock, & Hodgson, 2008)	Beliefs about self and others that are related to trust, safety, control, intimacy, and esteem.	84-item self-report measure with a 3rd grade reading level for ages 9 and up that takes 15 minutes to complete, and 5 minutes to score with an autoscore form. Prior experience in psychological testing and interpretation is required. T scores greater than 60 are considered to be high scores of disruption.	Acceptable test-retest reliability for subscales (r = .60–.79) and for total score (.75). Acceptable internal consistency (α = .67–.96).	Convergent and concurrent validity demonstrated in clinical and nonclinical samples. Discriminant validity and factorial validity demonstrated in nonclinical samples. Sensitivity demonstrated in clinical samples. Predictive and postdictive validity demonstrated.

Process

The suggested process would be to administer the SPTSS at intake in order to assess the presence of post-traumatic stress and symptoms. Its brevity, low reading level, and ability to assess those with possible multiple traumas make it ideal for assessing baseline and ongoing post-traumatic symptoms. Symptom severity and progress would then be examined with this measure every four sessions. This may help clinicians see how well clients are tolerating treatment. Along with the SPTSS, the HAq-II could be given every four sessions to assess the therapeutic alliance. This would provide a way for the therapist to address any ruptures and make efforts to improve the relationship given the role of the therapeutic alliance in bolstering treatment efficacy (Mulhauser, 2006).

Appendix A
SPTSS

In the Blank Space Before Each Question, Put a Number to Tell How Much that Thing Has Happened to You in the Past Week.

0 = not at all
1 = 1 or 2 times
2 = almost every day
3 = about once every day
4 = more than once every day

_____ 1. I don't feel like doing things that I used to like doing.
_____ 2. I can't remember much about bad things that have happened to me.
_____ 3. I feel cut off and isolated from other people.
_____ 4. I try not to think about things that remind me of something bad that happened to me.
_____ 5. I feel numb: I don't feel emotions as strongly as I used to.
_____ 6. I have trouble concentrating on things or paying attention to something for a long time.
_____ 7. I have a hard time thinking about the future and believing that I'm going to live to old age.
_____ 8. I feel very irritable and lose my temper.
_____ 9. I avoid doing things or being in situations that might remind me of something terrible that happened to me in the past.
_____ 10. I am very aware of my surroundings and nervous about what's going on around me.
_____ 11. I find myself remembering bad things that happened to me over and over, even when I don't want to think about them.
_____ 12. I get startled or surprised very easily and "jump" when I hear a sudden sound.
_____ 13. I have bad dreams about terrible things that happened to me.
_____ 14. I get very upset when something reminds me of something bad that happened to me.
_____ 15. I have trouble getting to sleep or staying asleep.

_____ 16. When something reminds me of something bad that happened to me, I feel shaky, sweaty, and nervous and my heart beats really fast.
_____ 17. I suddenly feel like I am back in the past, in a bad situation that I was once in, and it's like it is happening all over again.

Appendix B
The Revised Helping Alliance Questionnaire (HAq-II)

Instructions: These are ways that a person may feel or behave in relation to another person—the therapist. Consider carefully your relationship with your therapist, and then mark each statement according to how strongly you agree or disagree. *Please mark every one.*

	Strongly Disagree	Disagree	Slightly Disagree	Slightly Agree	Agree	Strongly Agree
1. I feel I can depend upon the therapist.	1	2	3	4	5	6
2. I feel the therapist understands me.	1	2	3	4	5	6
3. I feel the therapist wants me to achieve my goals.	1	2	3	4	5	6
4. At times I distrust the therapist's judgment.	1	2	3	4	5	6
5. I feel I am working together with the therapist in a joint effort.	1	2	3	4	5	6
6. I believe we have similar ideas about the nature of my problems.	1	2	3	4	5	6

(*Continued*)

	Strongly Disagree	Disagree	Slightly Disagree	Slightly Agree	Agree	Strongly Agree
7. I generally respect the therapist's views about me.	1	2	3	4	5	6
8. The procedures used in my therapy are not well suited to my needs.	1	2	3	4	5	6
9. I like the therapist as a person.	1	2	3	4	5	6
10. In most sessions, the therapist and I find a way to work on my problems together.	1	2	3	4	5	6
11. The therapist relates to me in ways that slow up the progress of the therapy.	1	2	3	4	5	6
12. A good relationship has formed with my therapist.	1	2	3	4	5	6
13. The therapist appears to be experienced in helping people.	1	2	3	4	5	6
14. I want very much to work out my problems.	1	2	3	4	5	6
15. The therapist and I have meaningful exchanges.	1	2	3	4	5	6

	Strongly Disagree	Disagree	Slightly Disagree	Slightly Agree	Agree	Strongly Agree
16. The therapist and I sometimes have unprofitable exchanges.	1	2	3	4	5	6
17. From time to time, we both talk about the same important events in my past.	1	2	3	4	5	6
18. I believe the therapist likes me as a person.	1	2	3	4	5	6
19. At times the therapist seems distant.	1	2	3	4	5	6

References

Adams, K. (1998). *The way of the journal: A journal therapy workbook for healing* (2nd ed.). Baltimore, MD: The Sidran Institute Press.
Ainsworth, M.D.S. (1979). Infant-mother attachment. *American Psychologist, 34* (10), 932–37. doi: 10.1037/0003-066X.34.10.932.
American Psychiatric Association. (2013). *Diagnostic and statistical manual of mental disorders* (5th ed.). Washington, DC: Author.
Amir, N., Stafford, J., Freshman, M.S., & Foa, E.B. (1998). Relationship between trauma narratives and trauma pathology. *Journal of Traumatic Stress, 11*(2), 385–92. doi: 10.1023/A:1024415523495.
Assagioli, R. (1967). *Jung and psychosynthesis: A series of three lectures given in 1966 at the Instituto di Psicosintesi, Florence, Italy*. New York, NY: Psychosynthesis Research Foundation.
Beck, J.S. (1995). *Cognitive therapy: Basics and beyond*. New York, NY: The Guilford Press.
Blake, D.D., Weathers, F.W., Nagy, L.M., Kaloupek, D.G., Gusman, F.D., Charney, D.S., et al. (1995). The development of a clinician-administered PTSD scale. *Journal of Traumatic Stress, 8*, 75–90. doi: 10.1002/jts.2490080106.
Boudewyns, P.A., & Hyer, L.A. (1990). Physiological response to combat memories and preliminary treatment outcome in Vietnam veteran PTSD patients treated with direct therapeutic exposure. *Behavior Therapy, 21*(1), 63–87. doi: 10.1016/S0005-7894(05)80189-3.
Bowen, G.R., & Lambert, J.A. (1986). Systematic desensitization therapy with posttraumatic stress disorder cases. In C.R. Figley (Ed.), *Trauma and its wake* (pp. 280–91). New York, NY: Brunner/Mazel.
Bowlby, J. (1977). The making and breaking of affectional bonds: I. Aetiology and psychopathology in light of attachment theory. *British Journal of Psychiatry, 130*, 201–10. doi: 10.1192/bjp.130.3.201.
Brewin, C.R., & Lennard, H. (1999). Effects of mode of writing on emotional narratives. *Journal of Traumatic Stress, 12*(2), 355–60. doi: 10.1023/A:1024736828322.
Briere, J. (2002). Treating adult survivors of severe childhood abuse and neglect: Further development of an integrative model. In J.E.B. Myers, L. Berliner, J. Briere, C.T. Hendrix, T. Reid, & C. Jenny (Eds.), *The APSAC handbook on child maltreatment* (2nd ed.) (pp. 1–26). Newbury Park, CA: Sage Publications.
Brown, E.J., & Heimberg, R.G. (2001). Effects of writing about rape: Evaluating Pennebaker's paradigm with a severe trauma. *Journal of Traumatic Stress, 14*(4), 781–90. doi: 10.1023/A:1013098307063.

References

Bryant, R.A., & Harvey, A.G. (2000). *Acute stress disorder: A handbook of theory, assessment, and treatment.* Washington, DC: American Psychological Association Press.

Bryant, R.A., Moulds, M., & Guthrie, R.M. (2001). Cognitive strategies and the resolution of acute stress disorder. *Journal of Traumatic Stress, 14*(1), 213–19. doi: 10.1023/A:1007856103389.

Bunting, K., & Hayes, S. (2008). Language and meaning: Acceptance and commitment therapy and the EI model. In K.J. Schneider (Ed.), *Existential-integrative psychotherapy: Guideposts to the core of practice* (pp. 217–34). New York, NY: Routledge.

Burton, C.M., & King, L.A. (2008). Effects of (very) brief writing on health: The two-minute miracle. *British Journal of Health Psychology, 13*, 9–14. doi: 10.1348/135910707X250910.

Cahill, S.P., Foa, E.B., Hembree, E.A., Marshall, R.D., & Nacash, N. (2006). Dissemination of exposure therapy in the treatment of posttraumatic stress disorder. *Journal of Traumatic Stress, 19*(5), 597–610. doi: 10.1002/jts.20173.

Carlson, E.B. (2001). Psychometric study of a brief screen for PTSD: Assessing the impact of multiple traumatic events. *Assessment, 8*(4), 431–441. doi: 10.1177/107319110100800408.

Carr, A. (1998). Michael White's narrative therapy. *Contemporary Family Therapy: An International Journal, 20*(4), 485–503.

Cason, D.R., Resick, P.A., & Weaver, T.L. (2002). Schematic integration of traumatic events. *Clinical Psychology Review, 22*(1), 131–53. doi: 10.1016/S0272-7358(01)00085-X.

Chavis, G.G. (2011). *Poetry and story therapy: The healing power of creative expression.* Philadelphia, PA: Jessica Kingsley Publishers.

Collins, K.S., Furman, R., & Langer, C.L. (2006). Poetry therapy as a tool of cognitively based practice. *The Arts in Psychotherapy, 33*, 180–87. doi: 10.1016/j.aip.2005.11.002.

Comas-Diaz, L. (2008). Latino psychospirituality. In K.J. Schneider (Ed.), *Existential-integrative psychotherapy: Guideposts to the core of practice* (pp. 100–109). New York, NY: Routledge.

Cook, J., Schnurr, P., & Foa, E. (2004). Bridging the gap between posttraumatic stress disorder research and clinical practice: The example of exposure therapy. *Psychotherapy: Theory, Research, Practice, Training, 41*(4), 374–87. doi: 10.1037/0033-3204.41.4.374.

Corsini, R.J. & Wedding, D. (2008). *Current psychotherapies.* Belmont: Thomson Brooks/Cole.

Curran, L.A. (2010). *Trauma competency: A clinician's guide.* Eau Claire, WI: PESI, LLC.

Dale, L.P., Carroll, L.E., Galen, G., Hayes, J.A., Webb, K.W., & Porges, S.W. (2009). Abuse history is related to autonomic regulation to mild exercise and psychological wellbeing. *Applied Psychophysiology and Biofeedback, 34*(4), 299–308. doi: 10.1007/s10484-009-9111-4.

Davidson, J.R., Rothbaum, B.O., van der Kolk, B.A., Sikes, C.R., & Farfel, G.M. (2001). Multicenter, double-blind comparison of sertraline and placebo in the treatment of posttraumatic stress disorder. *Archives of General Psychiatry, 58*, 485–92.

Davidson, J.R.T., Stein, D.J., Shalev, A.Y., & Yehuda, R. (2004). Posttraumatic stress disorder: Acquisition, recognition, course, and treatment. *Journal of Neuropsychiatry and Clinical Neurosciences, 16*(2), 135–47.

Davis, J.L., Petretic-Jackson, P.A., & Ting, L. (2001). Intimacy dysfunction and trauma symptomatology: Long-term correlates of different types of child abuse. *Journal of Traumatic Stress, 14*(1), 63–79.
De Francis, V. (1969). *Protecting the child victim of sex crimes committed by adults.* Denver, CO: American Humane Association.
de Shazer, S., Dolan, Y., Korman, H., Trepper, T., McCollum, E., & Berg, I.K. (2007). *More than miracles: The state of the art of solution-focused brief therapy.* New York, NY: Haworth Press.
Dickinson, E. (1993). *Collected poems.* New York, NY: Barnes and Noble Books.
Dieperink, M., Leskela, J., Thuras, P., & Engdahl, B. (2001). Attachment style classification and posttraumatic stress disorder in former prisoners of war. *American Journal of Orthopsychiatry, 71*(3), 374–78.
Elliott, D.E., Bjelajac, P., Fallot, R.D., Markoff, L.S., & Reed, B.G. (2005). Trauma-informed or trauma-denied: Principles and implementation of trauma-informed services for women. *Journal of Community Psychology, 33*(4), 461–77. doi: 10.1002/jcop.20063.
Fallot, R.D., & Harris, M. (2002). The trauma recovery and empowerment model (TREM): Conceptual and practical issues in a group intervention for women. *Community Mental Health Journal, 38*(6), 475–84.
Fehr, B. (2004). Intimacy expectations in same-sex friendships: A prototype interaction-pattern model. *Journal of Personality and Social Psychology, 86*(2), 265–84.
Fernández, I., & Paez, D. (2008). The benefits of expressive writing after the Madrid terrorist attack: Implications for emotional activation and positive affect. *British Journal of Health Psychology, 13*(1), 31–34. doi: 10.1348/135910707X251234.
Firman, J., & Gila, A. (2010). *A psychotherapy of love: Psychosynthesis in practice.* Albany, NY: State University of New York Press.
Foa, E.B., & Cahill, S.P. (2002). Specialized treatment for PTSD: Matching survivors to the appropriate modality. In R. Yehuda (Ed.), *Treating trauma survivors with PTSD: Bridging the gap between intervention research and practice* (pp. 43–62). Washington, DC: American Psychiatric Press.
Foa, E.B., Cahill, S.P., & Pontoski, K. (2004). Factors that enhance treatment outcome of cognitive-behavioral therapy for anxiety disorders. *The International Journal of Neuropsychiatric Medicine, 9*(14), 6–17, 35.
Foa, E.B., Ehlers, A., Clark, D.M., Tolin, D.F., & Orsillo, S.M. (1999). The Posttraumatic Cognitions Inventory (PTCI): Development and validation. *Psychological Assessment, 11*(3), 303–14.
Foa, E.B., & Meadows, E.A. (1997). Psychosocial treatments for Posttraumatic Stress Disorder: A critical review. *Annual Review of Psychology, 48,* 449–80.
Foa, E.B., & Rothbaum, B.O. (1998). *Treating the trauma of rape.* New York, NY: Guilford.
Foa, E.B., Rothbaum, B.O., & Furr, J.M. (2003). Augmenting exposure therapy with other CBT procedures. *Psychiatric Annals, 33*(1), 47–53.
Foa, E.B., Zoellner, L.A., Feeny, N.C., Hembree, E.A., & Alvarez-Conrad, J. (2002). Does imaginal exposure exacerbate PTSD symptoms? *Journal of Counseling and Clinical Psychology, 70*(4), 1022–28.
Ford, J.D., Courtois, C.A., Steele, K., van der Hart, O., & Nijenhuis, E.R.S. (2005). Treatment of complex posttraumatic self-dysregulation. *Journal of Traumatic Stress, 18*(5), 437–47.
Ford, J.D., & Russo, E. (2006). Trauma-focused, present-centered, emotional self-regulation approach to integrated treatment for posttraumatic stress and

addiction: Trauma adaptive recovery group education and therapy (TARGET). *American Journal of Psychotherapy, 60*(4), 335–54.

Ford, J.D., Russo, E.M., & Mallon, S.D. (2007). Integrating treatment of posttraumatic stress disorder and substance use disorder. *Journal of Counseling & Development, 85*, 475–88.

Ford, J.D., & Smith, S.F. (2008). Complex posttraumatic stress disorder in trauma-exposed adults receiving public sector outpatient substance abuse disorder treatment. *Addiction Research and Theory, 16*(2), 193–203. doi: 10.1080/16066350701615078.

Frank, E., Anderson, B., Stewart, B.D., Dancu, C., Hughes, C., & West, D. (1988). Efficacy of cognitive behavior therapy and systematic desensitization in the treatment of rape trauma. *Behavior Therapy, 19*, 403–20.

Furman, R. (2004). Exploring friendship loss through poetry. *Journal of Loss and Trauma, 9*(2), 181–87.

Furman, R. (2003). Poetry therapy and existential practice. *The Arts in Psychotherapy, 30*, 195–200. doi: 10.1016/S0197-4556(03)00052-2.

Gerard, R. (1961). *Psychosynthesis: A psychotherapy for the whole man*. New York, NY: Psychosynthesis Research Foundation.

Gorelick, K. (2005). Poetry therapy. In C.A. Malchiodi (Ed.), *Expressive Therapies* (pp. 117–40). New York, NY: Guilford Press.

Grame, C.J., Tortorici, J.S., Healey, B.J., Dillingham, J.H., & Winklebaur, P. (1999). Addressing spiritual and religious issues of clients with a history of psychological trauma. *Bulletin of the Menninger Clinic, 63*(2), 223–39.

Guastella, A.J., & Dadds, M.R. (2006). Cognitive-behavioral models of emotional writing: A validation study. *Cognitive Therapy Research, 30*, 397–414. doi: 10.1007/s10608-006-9045-6.

Guterman, J.T., & Rudes, J. (2005). A narrative approach to strategic eclecticism. *Journal of Mental Health Counseling, 27*(1), 1–12.

Harris, H.N., & Valentiner, D.P. (2002). World assumptions, sexual assault, depression, and fearful attitudes toward relationships. *Journal of Interpersonal Violence, 17*(3), 286–305.

Harrower, M. (1972). *The therapy of poetry*. Springfield, IL: Charles C. Thomas.

Herman, J. (1992). *Trauma and recovery*. New York, NY: Basic Books.

Honos-Webb, L., Sunwolf, Hart, S., & Scalise, J.T. (2006). How to help after national catastrophes: Findings following 9/11. *The Humanistic Psychologist, 34*(1), 75–97. doi: 10.1207/s15473333thp3401_7.

Hopper, J.W., Frewen, P.A., van der Kolk, B.A., & Lanius, R.A. (2007). Neural correlates of reexperiencing, avoidance, and dissociation in PTSD: Symptom dimensions and emotion dysregulation in responses to script-driven trauma imagery. *Journal of Traumatic Stress, 20*(5), 713–25. doi: 10.1002/jts.20284.

Hynes, A.M., & Hynes-Berry, M. (2011). *Biblio/poetry therapy: A handbook*. St. Cloud, MN: North Star Press of St. Cloud, Inc.

Ippen, C.G., & Kulkarni, M. (2005, June 8). *Trauma and Attachment Belief Scale (TABS)*. Retrieved from http://www.nctsnet.org/sites/default/files/assets/pdfs/measures/TABS_0.pdf.

Janoff-Bulman, R. (1989). Assumptive worlds and the stress of traumatic events: Applications of the schema construct. *Social Cognition, 7*(2), 113–36.

Janoff-Bulman, R. & Frieze, I.H. (1983). A theoretical perspective for understanding reactions to victimization. *Journal of Social Issues, 39*(2), 1–17. doi: 10.1111/j.1540-4560.1983.tb00138.x.

Kalay, E., Vaida, S., Borla, S., & Opre, A. (2008). The benefits of classic and enhanced tasks of expressive writing for the emotional life of female freshman students: A pilot study. *Cognition, Brain, Behavior, 12*(3), 251–64.

Kloss, J.D., & Lisman, S.A. (2002). An exposure-based examination of the effects of written emotional disclosure. *British Journal of Health Psychology, 7*, 31–46. doi: 10.1348/135910702169349.

Lamb, W. (2003). *Couldn't keep it to myself: Testimonies from our imprisoned sisters*. New York, NY: Regan Books.

Lee, C. (2004). Agency and purpose in narrative therapy: Questioning the postmodern rejection of metanarrative. *Journal of Psychology and Theology, 32*(3), 221–31.

Lerner, A. (1997). A look at poetry therapy. *The Arts in Psychotherapy, 24*(1), 81–89. doi: 10.1016/S0197-4556(96)00055-X.

Lerner, A. (1991). Some semantic considerations in poetry therapy. *Et Cetera*, 213–19.

Lindy, J.D. (1996). Psychoanalytic psychotherapy of posttraumatic stress disorder: The nature of the therapeutic relationship. In B.A. van der Kolk, A.C. McFarlane, & L. Weisaeth (Eds.), *Traumatic stress: The effects of overwhelming experience on mind, body, and society* (pp. 525–36). New York, NY: The Guilford Press.

Linehan, M. M. (1993). *Cognitive behavioral treatment of borderline personality disorder*. New York, NY: Guilford Press.

Luborsky, L., Barber, J.P., Siqueland, L., Johnson, S., Najavits, L.M., Frank, A., & Daley, D. (1996). The revised helping alliance questionnaire (HAq-II): Psychometric properties. *Journal of Psychotherapy Practice and Research, 5*(3), 260–71.

Maeve, M.K. (2000). Speaking unavoidable truths: Understanding early childhood sexual and physical violence among women in prison. *Issues in Mental Health Nursing, 21*(5), 473- 98. doi: 10.1080/01612840050044249.

Magnavita, J.J. (2005). *Personality-guided relational psychotherapy: A unified approach*. Washington, DC: American Psychological Association.

Main, M., & Morgan, H. (1996). Disorganization and disorientation in infant strange situation behavior: Phenotypic resemblance to dissociative states. In L.K. Michelson & W.J. Ray (Eds.), *Handbook of dissociation: Theoretical, empirical, and clinical perspectives* (pp. 107–38). New York, NY: Plenum Press.

Marshall, R.D., Beebe, K.L., Oldham, M., & Zaninelli, R. (2001). Efficacy and safety of paroxetine treatment for chronic PTSD: A fixed-dose-placebo-controlled study. *American Journal of Psychiatry, 158*, 1982–88. doi: 10.1176/appi.ajp.158.12.1982.

Mazza, N. (1999). *Poetry therapy: Interface of the arts and psychology*. New York, NY: CRC Press.

McArdle, S., & Byrt, R. (2001). Fiction, poetry and mental health: Expressive and therapeutic uses of literature. *Journal of Psychiatric and Mental Health Nursing, 8*, 517–24. doi: 10.1046/j.1351-0126.2001.00428.x.

McCabe, B. (2014, June). Mightier than the sword. *Johns Hopkins Magazine*. Retrieved from http://hub.jhu.edu/magazine/2014/summer/veterans-writing-project.

McCann, I.L., & Pearlman, L.A. (1990). *Psychological trauma & the adult survivor: Theory, therapy, and transformation*. New York, NY: Brunner/Mazel.

McCann, I.L., Sakheim, D.K., & Abrahamson, D.J. (1988). Trauma and victimization: A model of psychological adaptation. *Counseling Psychologist, 16*(4), 531–594. doi: 10.1177/0011000088164002.

McEwan, S.L., de Man, A.F, & Simpson-Housley, P. (2002). Ego-identity achievement and perception of risk in intimacy in survivors of stranger and acquaintance rape. *Sex Roles, 47*(5,6), 281–87. doi: 10.1023/A:1021390828178.

Meichenbaum, D. (1974). Self-instructional methods. In F.H. Kanfer & A.P. Goldstein (Eds.), *Helping people change* (pp. 357–91). New York, NY: Pergamon Press.

Miller, G.E., Chen, E., & Zhou, E.S. (2007). If it goes up, must it come down? Chronic stress and the hypothalamic pituitary-adrenocortical axis in humans. *Psychological Bulletin, 133*(1), 25–45. doi: 10.1037/0033-2909.133.1.25.

Miller, S.D., & Hubble, M.A. (2004). Further archeological and ethnological findings on the obscure, late 20th century, quasi-religious earth group known as "the therapists" (A fantasy about the future of psychotherapy). *Journal of Psychotherapy Integration, 14*(1), 38–65. doi: 10.1037/1053-0479.14.1.38.

Monson, C.M., Schnurr, P.P., Resick, P.A., Friedman, M.J., Young-Xu, Y., & Stevens, S.P. (2006). Cognitive Processing Therapy for veterans with military-related posttraumatic stress disorder. *Journal of Consulting and Clinical Psychology, 74*(5), 898–907. doi: 10.1037/0022-006X.74.5.898.

Mulhauser, G. (Ed.) (2006, August 9). The heart and soul of change: What works in therapy. [Review of the book *The heart and soul of change: What works in therapy*, edited by M.A. Hubble, B.L. Duncan, & S.D. Miller]. Retrieved from http://counsellingresource.com/books/what-works/.

Mulick, P.S., Landes, S.J., & Kanter, J.W. (2005). Contextual behavior therapies in the treatment of PTSD: A review. *International Journal of Behavioral Consultation and Therapy, 1*(3), 223–38.

Najavits, L.M. (2002). *Seeking safety: A treatment manual for PTSD and substance abuse*. New York, NY: The Guilford Press.

Najavits, L.M., Schmitz, M., Gotthardt, S., & Weiss, R.D. (2005). Seeking safety plus exposure therapy: An outcome study on dual diagnosis men. *Journal of Psychoactive Drugs, 37*(4), 425–33. doi: 10.1080/02791072.2005.10399816.

Najavits, L.M., Weiss, R.D., Shaw, S.R., & Muenz, L.R. (1998). "Seeking safety:" Outcome of a new cognitive-behavioral psychotherapy for women with posttraumatic stress disorder and substance dependence. *Journal of Traumatic Stress, 11*(3), 437–53. doi: 10.1023/A:1024496427434.

Neimeyer, R.A. (1999). Narrative strategies in grief therapy. *Journal of Constructivist Psychology, 12*, 65–85. doi: 10.1080/107205399266226.

O'Cleirigh, C., Ironson, G., Fletcher, M.A., & Schneiderman, N. (2008). Written emotional disclosure and processing of trauma are associated with protected health status and immunity in people living with HIV/AIDS. *British Journal of Health Psychology, 13*(1), 81–84. doi: 10.1348/135910707X250884.

O'Connor, M., Nikoletti, S., Kristjanson, L.J., Loh, R., & Willcock, B. (2003). Writing therapy for the bereaved: Evaluation of an intervention. *Journal of Palliative Medicine, 6*(2), 195–204. doi: 10.1089/109662103764978443.

Onyut, L.P., Neuner, F., Schauer, E., Ertl, V., Odenwald, M., Schauer, M. et al. (2005). Narrative exposure therapy as a treatment for child war survivors with posttraumatic stress disorder: Two case reports and a pilot study in an African refugee settlement. *BioMed Central Psychiatry, 5*(7), 1–9. doi: 10.1186/1471-244X-5-7.

Owens, G.P., & Chard, K.M. (2001). Cognitive distortions among women reporting childhood sexual abuse. *Journal of Interpersonal Violence, 16*(2), 178–91. doi: 10.1177/088626001016002006.

Park, C.L., & Blumberg, C.J. (2002). Disclosing trauma through writing: Testing the meaning-making hypothesis. *Cognitive Therapy and Research, 26*(5), 597–616. doi: 10.1023/A:1020353109229.

Pearlman, L. (2003). *Trauma and Attachment Belief Scale*. Los Angeles, CA: Western Psychological Services.
Pearlman, L. A. (2001). Treatment of persons with complex PTSD and other trauma-related disruptions of the self. In J.P. Wilson, M.J. Friedman, & J.D. Lindy (Eds.), *Treating psychological trauma & PTSD* (pp. 205–36). New York, NY: Guilford Press.
Pearlman, L.A., & Saakvitne, K.W. (1995). *Trauma and the therapist: Countertransference and vicarious traumatization in psychotherapy with incest survivors*. New York, NY: W.W. Norton & Company.
Pelcovitz, D., van der Kolk, B.A., Roth, S., Mandel, F., Kaplan, S., & Resick, P. (1997). Development of a criteria set and a structured interview for disorders of extreme stress (SIDES). *Journal of Traumatic Stress, 10*, 3–16. doi: 10.1023/A:1024800212070.
Peniston, E.G., & Kulkosky, P.J. (1991). Alpha-theta brainwave neuro-feedback therapy for Vietnam veterans with combat-related post-traumatic stress disorder. *Medical Psychotherapy, 4*, 47–60.
Penn, P. (2001). Chronic illness: Trauma, language, and writing: Breaking the silence. *Family Process, 40*(1), 33–52. doi: 10.1111/j.1545-5300.2001.4010100033.x.
Pennebaker, J.W. (2004). *Writing to heal: A guided journal for recovering from trauma and emotional upheaval*. Oakland, CA: New Harbinger Publications, Inc.
Pennebaker, J.W., Hughes, C.F., & O'Heeron, R.C. (1987). The psychophysiology of confession: Linking inhibitory and psychosomatic processes. *Journal of Personality and Social Psychology, 52*(4), 781–93. doi:10.1037/0022-3514.52.4.781.
Pennebaker, J.W., & Seagal, J.D. (1999). Forming a story: The health benefits of narrative. *Journal of Clinical Psychology, 55*(10), 1243–54. doi: 10.1002/(SICI)1097-4679(199910)55:10<1243::AID-JCLP6>3.0.CO;2-N.
Petersen, S., Bull, C., Propst, O., Dettinger, S., & Detwiler, L. (2005). Narrative therapy to prevent illness-related stress disorder. *Journal of Counseling & Development, 83*, 41–46. doi: 10.1002/j.1556-6678.2005.tb00578.x.
Pitman, R.K., Altman, B., Greenwald, E., & Longpre, R.E. (1991). Psychiatric complications during flooding therapy for posttraumatic stress disorder. *Journal of Clinical Psychiatry, 52*(1), 17–20.
Pole, N. (2007). The psychophysiology of posttraumatic stress disorder: A meta-analysis. *Psychological Bulletin, 133*(5), 725–46. doi: 10.1037/0033-2909.133.5.725.
Porges, S. (May, 2004). Neuroception: A subconscious system for detecting threats and safety. *Zero to Three*, 19–24. Retrieved from: http://www.lifespanlearn.org/documents/Porges- Neuroception.pdf.
Resick, P.A., & Schnicke, M.K. (1993). *Cognitive processing therapy for rape victims: A treatment manual*. Newbury Park, CA: Sage.
Rice, D. L. (2008). An African-American perspective: The case of Darrin. In K.J. Schneider (Ed.), *Existential-integrative psychotherapy: Guideposts to the core of practice* (pp. 110–21). New York, NY: Routledge.
Rojcewicz, S. (1999). Medicine and poetry: The state of the art of poetry therapy. *The International Journal of Arts Medicine, 6*(2), 4–9.
Rothbaum, B.O., Meadows, E.A., Resick, P., & Foy, D.W. (2000). Cognitive-behavioral therapy. In E.B. Foa, T.M. Keane, & M.J. Friedman (Eds.), *Effective treatments for PTSD: Practice guidelines from the International Society for Traumatic Stress Studies* (pp. 60–83). New York, NY: Guilford.
Rothschild, B. (2000). *The body remembers: The psychopathology of trauma and trauma treatment*. New York,, NY: W.W. Norton & Company.

Rottenberg, J., Salomon, K., Gross, J.J., & Gotlib, I.H. (2005). Vagal withdrawal to a sad film predicts subsequent recovery from depression. *Psychophysiology, 42*(3), 277–81. doi: 10.1111/j.1469-8986.2005.00289.x.

Sanderson, C.A., Rahm, K.B., Beigbeder, S.A., & Metts, S. (2005). The link between the pursuit of intimacy goals and satisfaction in close same-sex friendships: An examination of the underlying processes. *Journal of Social and Personal Relationships, 22*(1), 75–98. doi: 10.1177/0265407505049322.

Schauer, M., Neuner, F., & Elbert, T. (2005). *Narrative exposure therapy: A short-term intervention for traumatic stress disorders after war, terror, or torture*. Ashland, OH: Hogrefe & Huber Publishers.

Schneider, K.J. (2008). *Existential-integrative psychotherapy: Guideposts to the core of practice*. K.J. Schneider. (Ed.). New York, NY: Routledge.

Schneider-Rosen, K., & Cicchetti, D. (1984). The relationship between affect and cognition in maltreated infants: Quality of attachment and the development of visual self-recognition. *Child Development, 55*(2), 648–58. doi: 10.2307/1129976.

Schnurr, P.P., Friedman, M.J., Engel, C.C., Foa, E.B., Shea, M.T., Chow, B.K. et al. (2007). Cognitive behavioral therapy for posttraumatic stress disorder in women: A randomized controlled trial. *Journal of the American Medical Association, 297*(8), 820–30. doi: 10.1001/jama.297.8.820.

Schottenbauer, M.A., Arnkoff, D.B., Glass, C.R., & Gray, S.H. (2006). Psychotherapy for PTSD in the community: Reported prototypical treatments. *Clinical Psychology and Psychotherapy, 13*, 108–22. doi: 10.1002/cpp.480.

Serlin, I. (2008). Women and the midlife crisis: The Anne Sexton complex. In K.J. Schneider (Ed.), *Existential-integrative psychotherapy: Guideposts to the core of practice* (pp. 146–163). New York, NY: Routledge.

Shapiro, F. (1995). *Eye movement desensitization and reprocessing: Basic principles, protocols, and procedures*. New York, NY: Guilford Press.

Shapiro, F. & Maxfield, L. (2002). Eye movement desensitization and reprocessing (EMDR): Information processing in the treatment of trauma. *Journal of Clinical Psychology, 58*(8), 933–46. doi: 10.1002/jclp.10068.

Silver, S.M., Rogers, S., & Russell, M. (2008). Eye movement desensitization and reprocessing (EMDR) in the treatment of war veterans. *Journal of Clinical Psychology, 64*(8), 947–57. doi: 10.1002/jclp.20510.

Smyth, J., & Helm, R. (2003). Focused expressive writing as self-help for stress and trauma. *Journal of Clinical Psychology, 59*(2) 227–36. doi: 10.1002/jclp.10144.

Smyth, J.M., Hockemeyer, J.R., & Tulloch, H. (2008). Expressive writing and post-traumatic stress disorder: Effects on trauma symptoms, mood states, and cortisol reactivity. *British Journal of Health Psychology, 13*(1), 85–93. doi: 10.1348/135910707X250866.

Smyth, J.M., & Pennebaker, J.W. (2008). Exploring the boundary conditions of expressive writing: In search of the right recipe. *British Journal of Health Psychology, 13*, 1–7. doi: 10.1348/135910707X260117.

Soper, B., & Von Bergen, C.W. (2001). Employment counseling and life stressors: Coping through expressive writing. *Journal of Employment Counseling, 38*(3), 150–60.

Speedy, J. (2000). The 'storied' helper: Narrative ideas and practices in counselling and psychotherapy. *The European Journal of Psychotherapy, Counselling, & Health, 3*(3), 361–74. doi: 10.1080/13642530010012011.

Stolorow, R.D. (2008). Autobiographical and theoretical reflections on the "Ontological Unconsciousness." In K.J. Schneider (Ed.), *Existential-integrative psychotherapy: Guideposts to the core of practice* (pp. 281–90). New York, NY: Routledge.

Streeck-Fischer, A., & van der Kolk, B.A. (2000). Down will come baby, cradle and all: Diagnostic and therapeutic implications of chronic trauma on child development. *Australian and New Zealand Journal of Psychiatry, 34*(6), 903–18. doi: 10.1080/000486700265.

Taylor, L.K., Weems, C.F., Costa, N.M., & Carrion, V.G. (2009). Loss and the experience of emotional distress in childhood. *Journal of Loss and Trauma, 14*, 1–16. doi: 10.1080/15325020802173843.

Tedeschi, R.G., & Calhoun, L.G. (1996). The Posttraumatic Growth Inventory: Measuring the positive legacy of trauma. *Journal of Traumatic Stress, 9*(3), 455–72. doi: 10.1002/jts.2490090305.

Terr, L. (1990). *Too scared to cry: Psychic trauma in childhood*. New York, NY: Basic Books.

van der Hart, O, Nijenhuis, E.R.S., & Steele, K. (2006). *The haunted self: Structural dissociation and the treatment of chronic traumatization*. New York, NY: W.W. Norton & Company, Inc.

van der Kolk, B.A. (2002). Posttraumatic therapy in the age of neuroscience. *Psychoanalytic Dialogues, 12*(3), 381–92. doi : 10.1080/10481881209348674.

van der Kolk, B.A., & Courtois, C.A. (Eds.) (2005). Editorial comments: Complex developmental trauma. *Journal of Traumatic Stress, 18*(5), 385–88. doi: 10.1002/jts.20046.

van der Kolk, B.A., & Fisler, R.E. (1994). Childhood abuse and neglect and loss of self- regulation. *Bulletin of the Menninger Clinic, 58*(2), 145–68.

van der Kolk, B.A., McFarlane, A.C., & van der Hart, O. (1996). A general approach to treatment of posttraumatic stress disorder. In B.A. van der Kolk, A.C. McFarlane, & L. Weisaeth (Eds.), *Traumatic stress: The effects of overwhelming experience on mind, body, and society* (pp. 417–40). New York, NY: Guilford Press.

van der Kolk, B.A., Roth, S., Pelcovitz, D., Sunday, S., & Spinazzola, J. (2005). Disorders of extreme stress: The empirical foundation of a complex adaptation to trauma. *Journal of Traumatic Stress, 18*(5), 389–99. doi: 10.1002/jts.20047.

van Emmerik, A.A.P., Kamphuis, J.H., & Emmelkamp, P.M.G. (2008). Treating acute stress disorder and posttraumatic stress disorder with cognitive behavioral therapy or structured writing therapy: A randomized controlled trial. *Psychotherapy and Psychosomatics, 77*(2), 93–100. doi: 10.1159/000112886.

Varra, E.M., Pearlman, L.A., Brock, K.J., & Hodgson, S.T. (2008). Factor analysis of the trauma and attachment belief scale: A measure of cognitive schema disruption related to traumatic stress. *Journal of Psychological Trauma, 7*(3), 185–96. doi: 10.1080/19322880802266813.

Wagner, A.W., & Linehan, M.M. (2006). Applications of DBT to PTSD and related problems. In V.C. Follette, & J.I. Ruzek (Eds.), *Cognitive Behavioral Therapies for Trauma* (pp. 117–45). New York, NY: The Guilford Press.

Wenninger, K., & Ehlers, A. (1998). Dysfunctional cognitions and adult psychological functioning in child sexual abuse survivors. *Journal of Traumatic Stress, 11*(2), 281–300. doi: 10.1023/A:1024451103931.

Wisconsin Relationship Education (2010). Emotion words list. Retrieved from http://www.wire.wisc.edu/quizzesnmore/Emotionwords.aspx.

Wolfe, J., Chrestman, K.R., Ouimette, P.C., Kaloupek, D., Harley, R.M., & Bucsela, M. (2000). Trauma-related psychophysiological reactivity in women exposed to war-zone stress. *Journal of Clinical Psychology,* 56(10), 1371–79. doi: 10.1002/1097-4679(200010)56:10<1371::AID-JCLP8>3.0.CO;2-X.

Wright, J.H., Basco, M.R., & Thase, M.E. (2006). *Learning cognitive-behavior therapy.* Washington, DC: American Psychiatric Publishing, Inc.

Zlotnick, C., & Pearlstein, T. (1997). Validation of the structured interview for disorders of extreme stress. *Comprehensive Psychiatry,* 38(4), 243–47. doi: 10.1016/S0010-440X(97)90033-X.

Index

accident trauma and view of the world 8–9
accomplishments, listing 45, 49, 52
acrostics 66–69; current feeling 67; current thoughts 68; family, friends and others 68–69; hopes for the future 69; my body/body part topic 67; therapy topic 67; what I have lost topic 68; "What's going on" topic 67
activity-based exercises 108–20; guided imagery 110–16; multimedia activities 116–17; relaxation exercises 108–10
acute stress disorder (ASD) 3
Adaptive Information Processing (AIP) model 24
adult milestone being described in a narrative 92
advanced exercises 91–105; essays and compositions 96–105; narratives 91–95
advocacy letters 80
anger 27–28, 56, 89, 100–1, 103–5; and working through using poems 70, 72
anxiety 6–7, 9–11, 15–21, 23, 26, 28, 35, 37–39, 46, 57, 88–89
arousal, excessive 2–3, 5–7, 10, 14, 17, 19, 26, 28–30, 34, 39, 43, 47, 54, 74, 88–89
art 2; expressing feelings through 116; and healing 31–32; therapy 23
ASD. *See* acute stress disorder (ASD)
asking for forgiveness in essays and compositions 105
attachment therapy 18
audiences and describing traumatic events to 101–2
autonomic nervous system arousal 5–6

balance and integration images 115
beginning exercises 47–76; acrostics and poems 66–73; five-minute "Sprints," 73–77; lists and clusters 47–56; sentence stems 56–66
beliefs 123–4; about self by using guided imagery 114; creation and reinterpretation of 14–23; restructuring maladaptive 2; and writing exercises 61
benefit-finding 38, 76, 96
bibliotherapy 30, 32–33, 36, 43
bilateral stimulation 17
biofeedback 14
body: awareness of sensations 60; engaging through drawing, painting, sculpting 119–20; of self in guided imagery 115; sensations as images 114–15; speaking with one's 88–89; as a symbol topic in poems 71; as a word cluster 55
bodywork 14, 24
brain impacted by trauma 2, 4, 5–10, 35
breathing, diaphragmatic 108–9
brief dynamic therapy 19

central nervous system impacted by trauma 6, 34
change mirroring in guided imagery 113
character sketches 85–87; exploration of parts of the self 85–86; family and intimate others 87; feeling as a character 86–87; how others see me 87; ideal person 87; people who make me mad 87; places, things, and events 87
childhood in a narrative 92
childhood trauma 4, 6, 8–10, 40, 88–89, 98
Clinician-Administered Post-traumatic Stress Disorder Scale (CAPS-1) 122, 124
clusters, word 53–56
cognitions 2–3, 23; effects of trauma 8–10; negative 8, 22, 57, 123–4

144 Index

cognitive-behavioral therapy (CBT) 15–18, 23, 24; and poetry therapy 36–37
cognitive restructuring 22; in poetry therapy 36–38
cognitive schemas impacted by trauma 8–10
cognitive therapy and writing 36–37, 47
colors, healing 111, 115
compassion 70–71; developing 102–3; for others as topic in poems 72–73
complex post-traumatic stress disorder 3–4
consciousness 4, 19, 85, 122–3; stream of consciousness writing 107; wholeness of 3
Constructivist Self Development Theory (CSDT) 8
continuous writing 44
control, lack of 99–100
coping with the problem topic in poems 72
creativity 31–32, 78; and death 40
current feelings: in acrostics 67; for five-minute "Sprints," 75–76
current problems and what's going on as topic for five-minute "Sprints," 76
current thoughts topic in acrostics 68

Dear Problem letters 79
"defining who I am" writing exercise 56–57
desensitization 23, 39, 117–18
desires and actions needed topic 52–53
desomatization of experience 7
detailed exposure using sentence stems exercises 65–66
Diagnostic and Statistical Manual of Mental Disorders (DSM) 3
dialectical behavioral therapy (DBT) 16
dialogues: with an emotion 88; with a lost loved one 90; with one's body 88–89; with one's spiritual self 89–90; with parts of the self 88; with a trauma memory 90
diaphragmatic breathing 108–9
Dickinson, Emily 71
direct traumatization 123
disclosure 10, 20, 34, 39, 79; to others as topic in poems 73; of traumatic events to different audiences 101–2
disorders of extreme stress not otherwise specified (DESNOS) 4, 11
dissociation 28, 34, 43, 46, 47, 85

distress 17–18, 24–29, 35–37, 48–49, 81, 88, 114; induced by trauma-focused writing 38–40
dominant stories 20
doorway to feeling imagery 111
drawing and engaging the body exercise 119–20
dual-diagnosis and exposure therapy 27–28

emotional catharsis 2
emotional expression and healing 32–33
emotional processing and writing 37, 39
emotional self-regulation 2, 4–6, 10–11, 14–23, 38–39, 43, 47
emotional symbols, visualizing 111
emotions: and associated symbolic images 111; awareness of 48; creating metaphors for 50–51; dialogue with 88; essays on positive 96–98; identifying milestones in 51; inability in labeling and expressing 4, 6–7; self control of 48
essays and compositions 96–105; asking for forgiveness 105; developing compassion 102–3; exceptions to the negatives in life 98–99; focus on others 101–5; focus on self 96–101; forgiving others 103–5; holding opposite ideas 100–1; on life choices 99–100; on positive emotions 96
eulogies 83–85; for events 84; for people 83–84; for places 84; for self 83; for things 84
events as a character sketch 87
exceptions identification as sentence stem exercise 65–66
exceptions to the negatives in life 98–99
expository writing 78
exposure: beginning using creative writing exercises 62–65; detailed 65–66; graded 30; imaginal 2, 16, 26, 39, 65–66; prolonged 27; to traumatic stimuli 2, 3; treated by expressive writing 37–38; types of for treating 14–22, 24–29
exposure therapy 7, 16, 26, 117–18; increasing guilt 27; modifying to specific traumas 25–30
expressive writing 8, 23. *See also* writing; adding process of

Index

meaning-making 36; aiding self-disclosure 10, 34; beginning exercises 47–77; case for trauma treatment 25–31; closing the session 45–46; decreasing trauma symptoms 35; desired outcomes 53–55; engaging the brain 34–35, 40; general guidelines 43–44; improving mood 35; improving physical health 35; improving role functioning and psychological well-being 35–36; salutary effects of 33–36; structuring writing activities during session 44–46; as trauma therapy 2–3, 31–41; treating fears of death and dissolution 40

expressive writing workbook: acrostics 66–69; activity-based exercises 108–20; advanced exercises 91–105; beginning exercises 47–77; character sketches 85–87; dialogues 88–90; essays and compositions 96–105; feeling lists 49–53; five-minute "Sprints," 73–77; free-writing exercises 106–7; general writing guidelines 43–44; generating lists and clusters of words 47–56; guided imagery 110–16; intermediate exercises 78–90; letters 78–81; lists and clusters 47–56; multimedia activities 116–17; narratives 91–95; obituaries and eulogies 81–85; poems 69–73; relaxation exercises 108–10; semiautomatic writing 106; sentence stems 56–66; into the stream writing 107; structuring client writing activities 44–46; therapy and desired outcomes 53–55; word clusters 53

Eye-Movement Desensitization and Reprocessing (EMDR) 17, 24; and exposure therapy 27–28

family 59, 61–65, 80–85, 95; as a character sketch 87; describing in a narrative 92; as topic in acrostics 68–69; as a word cluster 55

family therapy 61

fear 5, 18, 38, 72, 82–83, 89, 111; of intimacy 9–10

feeling lists 49–53

feeling poems 70

feelings: as a character 86–87; doorway to imagery 111; expressing through art 116; as five-minute "Sprints," 75–76; as a word cluster 55

feelings profiles 59–60

fight-or-flight behaviors 7, 20

five-minute "Sprints," 73–77; current feelings as topic 75–76; current problems as topic 76; experience of therapy as topic 75; grounding questions as topic 74; hopes and finding life meaning as topic 76–77; rationale for 73–74; review of the day as topic 74–75; what I wish would have happened as topic 76

focus 60–63, 66–67, 70, 85, 94; on others 55, 62, 101–5; on past, present, and future 14–22, 63; on self 55, 92, 96–101; on trauma 93–95

forgiveness: asking for 105; in essays and compositions 103–5; as a word cluster 56

free association 23

freedom, personal 99–100

free-writing exercises 106–7; semiautomatic 106; into the stream 107

friends 34, 59, 68, 70, 87, 92–95, 101–3; described in a narrative 92

frontal lobe dysfunctioning 6

future: described in a narrative 95; focus on 14–22, 51–52, 55, 61, 63, 66–70, 76, 79–80, 83, 94–95

general feeling poems 70

"getting to heart of the matter" imagery 111

goals as a sentence stem exercise 64–65

gratitude and future focus 51–52

grief 26, 41, 59, 63–64, 95, 103–4, 111, 116; and guided imagery 112; and loss as a word cluster 55–56; working through using poems 71

guided imagery 110–16; body sensations as images 114–15; doorway to feeling 111; facilitating grieving 112; getting to the heart of the matter 111; healing colors 111, 115; images of integration and balance 115; images of light 115–16; imagining a different outcome 114; meeting with you again 112; mirroring change 113; my body as myself 115; my ideal activities and behaviors 113–14; reconstructing the self 114; reflection of myself 114; safety-centering 110–11; unifying centers 112–13; visualizing

a traumatic memory 114; visualizing emotional symbols 111
guilt 10, 22, 80, 100; increased by exposure therapy 27; as a word cluster 56

habituation 20, 23, 26
happiness as a sentence stem exercise 64
healing colors in guided imagery 111, 115
holiday cards 78
hope: described in a narrative 95; and finding life meaning as topic for five-minute "Sprints," 76–77; for the future topic in acrostics 69; as a symbol topic in poems 71; as a word cluster 55
how others see me topic 87
hyper-arousal of traumatic stress 3, 5–7, 10, 28–29, 43; induced by trauma-focused writing 38
hypnotherapy 19, 23

ideal person as a character sketch 87
ideas, opposite 100–1
identity and meaning exploration 58–59
"If I should be" topic in writing exercises 61
imagery, guided 110–16
images: and associated emotions 111; body sensations as 114–15; of light 115–16
imaginal exposure 2, 16, 26, 39, 65–66
imaging a different outcome 114
important people as a word cluster 55
impulse control, impaired 6, 7
inner guide 89–90
Inner Wisdom 90
insight 96
integration and balance images 115
integrative therapy 1–2
intermediate exercises 78–90; character sketches 85–87; dialogues 88–90; obituaries and eulogies 81–85; writing letters 78–81
Internal Self-Helper 90
interpersonal effects of trauma 8–10
interpersonal problems 47
interpersonal trauma and view of the world 8–9
intimacy 8–11, 40, 61, 125; decreased level of 8–10; fear of 9–10
intimate others: as a character sketch 87; describing in a narrative 92

into the stream writing 107
in vivo exposure 16
I wish topic in writing exercises 61

journaling 35

letters 78–81; accepting trauma 81; advocacy 80; Dear Problem letters 79; holiday cards 78; to important others 79–80; to self 79
life 15–16, 20–21, 28, 36, 51–53, 59–73, 81–86, 97–99, 103–5, 112–14; and finding meaning in 8, 33, 76–77
life choices in essays and compositions 99–100
life space 48
light, images of 115–16
lists: about lists 48–49; about personal positives 49; about therapy 49; based on the Miracle Question 52–53; and clusters of words 47–56; feeling 49–53
long-handed writing narrative of traumatic experience 39
loss 34, 40, 55, 63–64, 71, 81–85, 95, 103, 105, 111, 116; topic in acrostics 68
lost loved one and talking with 90

Madrid terrorist attack 35
maladaptive beliefs 2, 7, 9, 23, 27–28, 86
meaningfulness of the world 8–9
meaning-making process 36
meeting with you again imagery 112
memory: conversation with traumatic 90; for integrating trauma with their lives 62–65; reorganizing 117; visualizing traumatic memory using guided imagery 114
mental health: and poetry therapy 36–38; and writing 33
metaphor: for emotions 50–51; to understand problems 71–72
Miracle Question 52–53
mirroring change imagery 113
mirror reflection writing exercise 118–19
mood improvement 35
multimedia activities 116–17; acting out a different outcome 117; confronting trauma triggers 118; engaging the body through drawing, painting, sculpting 119–20; exposure to trauma objects 117–18; expressing

feelings through art 116; mirror reflection writing exercise 118–19; music reflection 116; role-plays using parts of the self 116–17
music reflection 116
my body as myself in guided imagery 115
my body/body part topic in acrostics 67
my body speaks writing exercise 60
my ideal activities and behaviors imagery 113–14
my loss as a sentence stem exercise 63–64

narratives 91–95; aftermath of trauma 95; an adult milestone 92; being a teen 92; childhood 92; family 92; focus on self 92; focus on trauma 93–95; friends and important others 93; future hopes 95; intimate others 92–93; reactions of others 95
narrative therapy 20, 30
negative cognitions 8, 22, 56, 123–4
negatives and describing exceptions to 98–99
neural activation in trauma re-experiencing 5
neurofeedback 14

obituaries 81–83; for others 82–83; for self 81–82
opposite ideas, holding 100–1
optimism 96
others: compassion for 72–73; disclosing to 73; focus on in essays and compositions 101–5; focus on in narratives 92–93; reactions of in narrative 95
outcome 7, 10, 20, 34, 53–56; acting out a different one 117; imagining a different one 114
outcome measures 121–6
over-arousal 3, 5–7, 10, 28–29; induced by trauma-focused writing 38

pacing and containment in writing activities during session 44–45
painting and engaging the body 119–20
past: correcting it 51; focus on 13–22, 31–32, 41, 74–75, 81–84, 94–95, 119
past, present, and future oriented exercises 24–25, 51–53, 63, 79, 99

"people who make me mad" as a character sketch 87
perceived benevolence of the world 8–9
Personal Beliefs and Reactions Scale 123
personal belief structure 61, 123
personal choice 94
personal freedom 99–100
personal island topic in poetry 69
personality 11, 47, 55; apparently normal part 85; conflicts in guided imagery 112–13; division of 85; emotional part 85; visualizing ideal activities and behaviors 113–14
personal positives, listing 49
personal quality as a word cluster 55
personal responsibility 99–100
personal strengths and coping 49
pharmacotherapy 15, 24
physical self-awareness 14–24
physiological arousal returning to diminished state 5–6, 34
places as a character sketch 87
play therapy 14, 18
poems 69–73; compassion for others 72–73; coping with the problem topic 72; disclosing to others topic 73; general feeling 70; personal island topic 69; pros and cons related to the problem topic 72; stable place topic 69; symbolized values/beliefs topic 71; understanding the problem topic 71–72; working through anger topic 70; working through grief topic 71
poetry therapy 2, 3, 31–33, 39; and cognitive restructuring 36–38
positive emotions in essays and compositions 96–98
postmodern/constructivist approach to treating post-traumatic stress disorder (PTSD) 20
Post-traumatic Cognitions Inventory (PTCI) 122, 123, 124
post-traumatic stress disorder (PTSD): and brain activity 5; case for expressive writing treatment 25–31; cognitive-behavioral therapy (CBT) approaches 15–18, 23, 24, 36; complex 3–4; defined 3; postmodern/constructivist approach to treating 20; psychodynamic approaches to treating 18–19, 24; psycho-physiological approaches to treating

14–15; screening for symptoms
  121–6; and substance abuse 1, 4;
  trauma-informed group treatments
  21–22; trauma narrative articulation
  7; treating 11, 14–22; treating by
  exposure therapy 27–28; treating by
  expressive writing 35–36
powerlessness 64, 89, 99–100
present as focus after writing 45
problem: coping with it via poems
  72; externalization of 79, 84, 86;
  identification with sentence stems
  exercises 63; pros and cons related
  to it 72; understanding it via poems
  71–72
progressive muscle relaxation (PMR)
  109–10
prolonged exposure 27
prompts for imagining a safe place
  writing exercise 56–57
pros and cons related to the problem as
  topic in poems 72
psychobiology of trauma 4–6
psychodynamic approaches to treating
  post-traumatic stress disorder (PTSD)
  18–19, 24
psychoeducation 17, 21, 28–29
psycho-physiological approaches
  to treating post-traumatic stress
  disorder (PTSD) 14–15
psychotherapy 1, 31–33, 36, 99, 113
PTSD. *See* post-traumatic stress
  disorder (PTSD)

questions for five-minute "Sprints," 74

rape trauma and exposure therapy 27
rapport: measuring with patient
  and therapist 121–2; therapist
  establishing with patient 47–48, 61
Rational Emotive and Behavioral
  Psychotherapy (REBT) and writing
  36–37
rational voice 2
reactions of others in a narrative 95
recall 65–66; and beginning exposure
  62–65
reconnecting with society and
  community 62
reflection of myself 114
reflection time after writing 44, 45
regulation of affect 14–23
reinterpretation and creation of new
  beliefs 14–23

relationships 6, 8–10, 18, 21, 58–59,
  69–70, 86–87, 94–102, 111–12;
  defining with others with sentence
  stems 61–62; and sentence stems
  61–62; visualized as images of
  integration and balance 115
relaxation exercises 108–10;
  diaphragmatic breathing 108–9;
  progressive muscle relaxation (PMR)
  109–10
representational memory 6, 11
responsibility, personal 99–100
restorying 20
re-traumatization 25, 29
review of the day for five-minute
  "Sprints," 74–75
Revised Helping Alliance Questionnaire
  (HAq-II) 121–22, 126, 129–31
right anterior insula 5
role-play using parts of the self 116–17

safe place, imagining 110–11
safety-centering 110–11
Screen for Post-traumatic Stress
  Symptoms (SPTSS) 121, 125–8
sculpting and engaging the body
  119–20
seeking safety treatment 21
self: control of emotions 48; dialogue
  with parts of the self 88; exploration
  of parts 85–86; focus of in essays
  and compositions 96–101; focus on
  in narratives 92; jump-start writing
  about 57; reconstructing using
  guided imagery 114; role-play using
  parts of the self 116–17; as a symbol/
  belief topic in poems 71; window
  into self 57–58; worthiness of 8–10
self-blame 8–10, 97, 123, 125
self-censorship 73
self-definition 58–59
self-disclosure. *See* disclosure
self-image 114, 119
self-regulation skills 2, 4–6
semiautomatic writing 106
semi-guided free association 62–65
sense of safety 2, 18, 44, 47
sentence stems 56–66; beliefs 61;
  defining who I am 56–57; detailed
  exposure 65–66; feelings profiles
  59–60; focus on others 62; happiness
  64; happiness, goals, and roadblocks
  64–65; identifying exceptions 65–66;
  identity and meaning exploration

58–59; If I could be 61; I wish 61; jump-start writing about the self 57; my body speaks 60; my loss 63–64; problem identification 63; prompts for imaging a safe place 56–57; recall and beginning exposure 62–65; relationship with others 61–62; trauma details 65; window into self 57–58
setting the writer free writing exercise 56
sexual abuse 4, 8–10, 88; treated by expressive writing 32, 40
shame 10, 22, 39, 73, 77; as a word cluster 56
"shoulds, oughts, and musts," 61
simile to understand problems 71–72
Solution-Focused Brief Therapy 52
spiritual self 89–90
spontaneity, maximizing 73
spontaneous recall 14–24
stable place topic in poetry 69
Stainbrook, Edward 3
stimuli tolerance of exposure to trauma 2, 3, 14–22, 24
story-markers 96
storytelling 35, 91–92
stream of consciousness writing 107
Stress Inoculation Training (SIT) 17
Structured Interview for Disorders of Extreme Stress (SIDES) 122, 125
Structured Writing Therapy (SWT) 37
subjective units of distress (SUDS) 17, 18, 26
substance abuse linked to trauma 1, 4
substance-use disorders (SUD) and exposure therapy 27–28
symbolized values/beliefs topic in poems 71
symbols 7, 31, 50, 71, 111–17
symptoms 2–11, 15, 17, 22, 25–41, 43, 57, 64, 73, 100, 103; associated 122; measuring PTSD 121–6
systemic desensitization 18

talk therapy 8, 10–11
teen describing being one in a narrative 92
therapeutic window 28, 29
therapist: establishing rapport with patient 47–48, 61; use for therapeutic writing 43–44, 47
therapy: See also specific types of therapy; drop-out rates 25–26; experience of for five-minute "Sprints," 75; topic in acrostics 67; types of 13–22
things as a character sketch 87
thoughts and beliefs as a word cluster 55
threat to survival 5
timeline of client's trauma history 14–22, 24
trauma: accepting 81; accident 8–9; aftermath described in a narrative 95; chronic and/or developmental 3–4; conversation with trauma memory 90; describing to different audiences 101–2; details using sentence stems exercises 65; effects 1–10; exposure to objects 117–18; externalization 96; focus on in a narrative 93–95; impacting the brain 2, 4, 5–10, 35; impact on central nervous system 6, 34; intergenerational effects 1; interpersonal 8–10; linked to substance abuse 1, 4; narrative articulation 7; processing aided by narrative construction 93; psychobiology 4–6; reappraisal of 37–38; re-experience and brain activity 5, 35; related triggers 63, 117–18; sharing effects of with others 79–80; topic of essays and compositions 96; treatments for 13–41; Type I 3; Type II 3; as a word cluster 56
Trauma Adaptive Recovery Group Education and Therapy (TARGET) 21, 29, 30
Trauma and Attachment Belief Scale (TABS) 122, 123, 125
trauma-informed group treatments for post-traumatic stress disorder (PTSD) 21–22
Trauma Recovery and Empowerment Model (TREM) 22
traumatization: direct 123; vicarious 123
trauma treatment 1, 121–6. See also specific types of therapy; and emotional regulation 10–11, 14–23, 38–39; expressive writing 30–41; impacted by reluctance to self-disclose 10; integrative therapy 1–2; multidimensional model of 23–25; psychotherapy 1
trusting states, lack of 5–6

Type II trauma 3
Type I trauma 3
typing the narrative of traumatic experience 39

"understanding the problem" topic in poems 71–72
unifying centers imagery 112–13
unique outcomes 20

vagal regulation, poor 5–6
verbal expression inability 4, 6–7
veterans 62, 118, 122; and exposure therapy 27; and expressive writing as therapy 30
vicarious traumatization 123
Vietnam veterans and exposure therapy 27
visualization: acquiring personal characteristics 113–14; emotional symbols 111; guided 110; images of integration and balance 115; somatic states in guided imagery 114–15; traumatic memory 114

"what I have lost" topic in acrostics 68
"what I wish would have happened" topic in five-minute "Sprints," 76
"What's going on" topic in acrostics 67
will and role of 94
Williams McPearl Belief Scale 40
window into self 57–58
wishing and imagining 61, 63
witnessing a traumatic event 59, 76, 95
word clusters 53–56; on desired personal quality 55; focus on important others 55; focus on self 55; focus on trauma 55–56; on hope 55; on main problems 54; on therapy 53
working through anger topic in poetry 70
working through grief topic in poetry 71
world 22, 39, 72, 76, 83, 123–4; meaningfulness of 8–9; perceived benevolence of 8–9; trauma-related beliefs about 61
World Assumptions Scale (WAS) 9
writing. *See also* expressive writing: about loss 81–85; exercises to treat PTSD 2; expository 78; in front of the mirror 118–19; jump starting writing about the self 57; semiautomatic 106; sprints 73–77; stream of consciousness 107